INTRODUCTION TO SCIENCE AND THE SCIENTIFIC METHOD

INTRODUCTION TO SCIENCE AND THE SCIENTIFIC METHOD

JOHN L. CAMPBELL

Kravitz & Sons

INNOVATORS IN PUBLISHING, MARKETING AND ADVERTISING

The excerpt from "UFOs, Horoscopes, Bigfoot, Psychics, and Other Nonsense" originally appeared in Smithsonian magazine, March 1978 and is reprinted herein by permission of the author, Kendrick Frazier.

Kravitz and Sons LLC
1301 Farmville Blvd, Suite 104
Greenville, NC 27834

Published by Kravitz and Sons LLC.

ISBN: 979-8-89639-234-7 (sc)
ISBN: 979-8-89639-235-4 (e)
ISBN   979-8-89639-236-1 (h)

Library of Congress Control Number: 2025906596

In the furtherance of understanding

PREFACE

Americans are continually exposed to and affected by scientific knowledge (scientific information) as well as to the many goods and services it permits. By scientific knowledge is meant the findings of research scientists and ideas of theoretical scientists. Also, it means findings and ideas of basic science (pure science) and of applied science, which is often indistinguishable from technology (engineering). People differ as to what and how much scientific information they possess, how well they understand it, how current it is, what they do with it, and what value they place on it. They differ, too, in what and how much they know about the method scientists use—the scientific method—for generating this information/knowledge. Casual conversation, radio and television news, newspaper and magazine articles, and popular books are informal ways the public learns about developments in science. Also they are the ways scientists stay abreast of scientific developments outside their increasingly specialized fields and subfields. Overall, the American public has become somewhat literate in, or knowledgeable of, science. However, nearly all the energy mustered for instilling scientific literacy has gone into acquainting people with scientific knowledge, not the scientific method. This is unfortunate and has furnished much of my reason for writing this book.

There seem to be two reasons for the skimpiness in making the public aware of the scientific method. One is a desire to take as little time as possible away from showing how much science knows and has done for society. Clearly, to show these things is to win support for science in general as well as for science education, science funding, and science-inspired technological, health, and social reforms in particular. The other reason is a feeling science's method is so boring or difficult to learn that instructing non-aspiring scientists in it is mostly a waste of time. Unfortunately, science and the public at large both suffer if the average citizen knows little about the scientific method. For ignorance of its method often leads to unrealistic hopes and expectations in what science can do, and these in turn frequently cause people to become unduly disillusioned with science's findings (scientific knowledge). Now a side benefit of having a public that is generally familiar with science's method is having people who are better able to know what is and isn't regarded by scientists to be scientific—something born of science—and to thereby be more adept at telling science from nonscience.

In what follows I give readers an introduction to science and the scientific method. Neither exists in a vacuum. They dovetail with, influence, and are influenced by philosophy, logic, mathematics, history, society, and even religion. Consequently, this book will make forays into these areas when doing so seems advisable. Still, the book's thrust is science and especially the scientific method. It should be said before going further that despite the scientific method employing procedures and techniques, it is more than a set of procedures and techniques. Rather, it's a general, flexible, and therefore versatile approach to knowing nature (basic science) and to knowing how to use nature (applied science). My hope is that when you finish the book you will feel you have been more than slightly enlightened.

John L. Campbell

Roseburg, OR 97470

January 2017*

----

*This is a revised edition. It removes ambiguities and errors in the July 2014 edition Also it omits chapter 4 (Statistical Analysis Of Research Data).

TABLE OF CONTENTS

CHAPTER 1

Getting To Know Science

Let us begin with a look at the word science. Science comes from the Latin word scientia, which means a body of systematized knowledge about something. Related to the word science is the word philosophy. Philosophy comes from the Greek word philosophos, meaning a person who loves (phil-) wisdom (sophia). What is the relationship between the words science and philosophy? Philosophy signifies not only knowing something well but being wise in it and hence possessing a deep insight into it or a profound understanding of it. We can thus say that to be wise is to know but to know is not necessarily to be wise. The words science and philosophy and their cognates (words stemming from them, such as scientist, scientifically, philosopher, and philosophically) are rough labels. Consequently the point at which the caliber of the knowledge about something stops being merely knowledge and starts being philosophy is hard, if not impossible, to specify. Yet we can sense a distinction between the two, and this helps us understand why there is such an activity as the philosophy of science. Basically, science generates knowledge and philosophy of science reflects upon that knowledge and its bases.

From more than two thousand years ago to roughly 1875 people spoke of a science or of sciences but not of science. The reason why is that what we know today as science was until then known as natural philosophy. Natural philosophy was one of a half-dozen branches of ancient and medieval philosophy, the branch which is devoted to generating knowledge about nature and the universe or, simply, nature. So besides the semantic relationship between science and philosophy just mentioned (i.e., what is meant by science and philosophy), we see a historical relationship between them: philosophy in the form of natural philosophy became known as science.

Prior to approximately 1875 the sciences and therefore the bodies of systematized knowledge about things had been associated with philosophy (i.e., the astronomy, physics, chemistry, and biology making up natural philosophy, along with philosophy's remaining branches of metaphysics, logic, epistemology, ethics, aesthetics, and newly conceived social philosophy) and with such professions and trades as medicine, jurisprudence (law), mathematics, geography, history, metallurgy, stone masonry, weaving, etc. After 1875, three things happened. First, natural philosophy was increasingly termed natural science. Second, social philosophy, which arose during the late 1700s, was increasingly termed social science. Therefore, science was increasingly seen to embrace natural science (formerly natural philosophy) and social science (formerly social philosophy). Third, a body of systematized knowledge about something was increasingly called a science only if it is one of the natural sciences (i.e., astronomy, physics, geology, chemistry, biology, paleontology, etc.) or social sciences (i.e., psychology, sociology, anthropology, economics, political science, etc.). Hence pursuits like metaphysics, logic, epistemology, ethics, aesthetics, medicine, jurisprudence, etc. were less often referred to as sciences after 1875.

As natural philosophy steadily became known as science, we see tensions brew between philosophically inclined natural scientists (the old guard) and social scientists (the newcomers) over 'the' method employed for generating 'all' scientific knowledge. Now differences in method had existed when science was no more than what natural philosophy had been; namely, astronomy, physics, chemistry, and biology. Yet the differences between how physicists generate knowledge and how biologists generate knowledge were viewed as minor and inconsequential. Not so for differences between how physicists generate knowledge and how anthropologists generate it. The onus was on social scientists to conform to the ways of natural scientists, and pressure to do this was brought to bear as much by social scientists themselves as by natural scientists. More than a few times during the late 1800s a sociologist, psychologist, or economist urged colleagues to generate their knowledge like natural scientists do. Often physics was touted as the model science, the ideal that all other sciences, particularly the social sciences, ought to emulate.

Around 1875 a few influential scientists began promoting a definition of science that came to be accepted by most natural scientists and many social scientists by about 1910:

> Science is the generation of knowledge (information) by means of the integrated utilization of research and theory.

This definition clarifies the meaning of science in terms of scientific knowledge and then clarifies the meaning of scientific knowledge in terms of the scientific method, which is implicitly addressed by the words *integrated utilization of research and theory*. Left unsaid is what's meant by research, by theory, and by their integrated utilization. To know these three things is to know the scientific method and, ultimately, science. But a firm understanding of them cannot be achieved by definition alone. Such comprehension takes time to instill and will consume many of the pages to follow.

It might be smart to digress awhile to gain some perspective on the history of natural philosophy. We'll adopt the practice of regarding prehistory as everything before roughly 3500 B.C., ancient history as going from 3500 B.C. to 400 A.D., medieval history as going from 400 (A.D.) to 1300, renaissance history as going from 1300 to 1600, and modern history as everything after 1600. Interest in nature (and the universe) arose long before the dawn of history and thus long before written records began to be kept. This is suggested by cave art and notches (tally marks?) carved on bone dating back to at least 30,000 B.C. Records concerning nature started to be kept by Sumerians about 3300 B.C., Egyptians about 3000 B.C., Babylonians and Chinese about 1850 B.C., Assyrians about 1100 B.C., Mayans and Chaldeans about 600 B.C., Greeks about 575 B.C., Romans about 200, and Hindus about 400. Unfortunately, those of these records which we have at our disposal are patchy.

Note that the patchiness of ancient records, be they about natural philosophy or anything else, is not due strictly to few being written. Less than 25% of all created have come down to us. Some turned to dust before being copied. Others perished in natural disasters. Still others were lost when destroyed for ideological reasons. This was the fate of countless scrolls and codices — the forerunners of our books — when braries of Alexandria in Egypt, Pergamon and Constantinople in Turkey, Carthage in Tunisia, and Autun in France were sacked. Alexandria's library, the biggest (estimated to have held up to 700,000 volumes), was hit three times: in the first century B.C. and in the fourth and seventh centuries. We have inherited a fragmentary picture of what was known in antiquity!

Knowing nature clearly involves observing nature and thinking about nature. A few say it also entails intuiting nature. Observing, or observation, is a general term. It means seeing, hearing, touching, smelling, tasting, sensing pain, sensing temperature, sensing bodily position, and other sensory/perceptual processes commonly termed our senses. Observations mean the results of these processes and therefore what we see, hear, touch, smell, taste, sense as pain, etc. Knowing nature by observing it generates what is called an empirical knowledge about nature, empirical signifying observation. Thinking is characterized as emotional, rational, abstract, concrete, subjective, objective, etc. Rational thinking interests us here. Such thinking uses reasoning, or reason, to link together in ways we consider meaningful the observations we make or the thoughts that pop into our mind, many thoughts stemming from observations. Knowing nature by reasoning about it generates a rational knowledge about nature. Finally, knowing nature by intuiting it generates an intuitive or mystical knowledge about nature. Intuiting, or intuition, is difficult to define. A few say intuition/mysticism is an extrasensory (a non-sensory) process. Since 1800, scientists have usually employed a blend of observation and reason in order to know about nature. Also since then they have ridiculed the use of intuition. Note that the words positivism, positivist, and positivistic were coined in the mid-1800s as synonyms for empiricism, empiricist, and empirical that imply observation is the best approach to knowing nature.

From 3300 B.C. to 1800, most natural philosophers sought empirical knowledge. In this respect they were more like today's research scientists than today's theoretical scientists. An exception was the many natural philosophers living in Greece between 575 and 275 B.C. They were oriented toward acquiring rational knowledge and thus were more akin to contemporary theoretical scientists than to contemporary research scientists. Yet these Greek philosophers were unlike contemporary theoretical scientists in that they relied on reason, not observation, to evaluate the correctness of their theories. Such rationalistic theories would nowadays be labeled speculations (e.g., Aristotle's astronomical theory) or models (e.g., Ptolemy's astronomical theory).

It should be realized that natural philosophy emerged in different places at different times. Like seeds alighting upon soil, it might germinate in a place or might not. If it did germinate, then it might endure or it might wither away, maybe to sprout again someday. Wherever natural philosophy endured, its orientation to studying nature would be heavily shaped by the worldview, interests, aspirations, and social values of the specific culture nurturing it. Natural philosophy was mainly a culture-specific activity or, if well enough organized, a culture-specific social institution until around 1600. At that time a reformation in natural philosophy commenced occurring in European cultures which about 1800 started spreading beyond Europe to become by 1925 the natural philosophy of all the world's advanced cultures. We know this reformed natural philosophy today as modern science and see its birth as having signaled a major change in how natural philosophy/science is done, a change so great as to be later heralded as the Scientific Revolution. The revolution erupted in Italy in 1600 and rumbled through France, Belgium, England, the Netherlands, and Germany between then and 1700.

Modem science — reformed natural philosophy — did not suddenly arise, full-blown Rather, it arose slowly between 1600 and 1800 as consensus among scientists regarding how science is to be performed was slowly reached, detail by detail. Perhaps the key detail on which consensus was needed is the relationship that ought to exist between observation and reason. Two extreme stances on this are possible. One is the extreme empiricist position that knowledge about nature ought to be based solely on observation. The other is the extreme rationalist position that knowledge about nature ought to be based solely on reason. Between these extremes are numerous intermediate stances. Implicit to extreme empiricism is that theory is nothing; implicit to extreme rationalism is that theory is everything. And implicit to theory being everything is that observation cannot be legitimately used to show a theory is wrong, despite earlier observations having inspired that theory's creation.

Stances mirroring each extreme arose around 1620 and 1635. First to arise was the empirical view of Englishman Francis Bacon, known as Bacon's empirical philosophy or Baconian empiricism. The second to appear was the rational view of the Frenchman Rene Descartes, called Descartes' rational philosophy or Cartesian rationalism. During the mid and late 1600s both viewpoints competed for support from the growing number of natural philosophers unhappy with how nature was portrayed by the ancient Greek philosopher Aristotle, whose far-ranging, largely rational philosophy was termed Aristotelian rationalism or simply Aristotelianism. Aristotelianism had been the prevailing body of European knowledge concerning nature ever since it was widely accepted in the early 1200s by Europe's bourgeoning intellectuals. During the late 1200s it was accepted with some reluctance by Roman Catholicism, upon the Roman Catholic Church adopting Saint Thomas Aquinas' philosophy (known as Thomistic philosophy or Thomism). Thomism was a reconciling of Aristotle's philosophy with Church doctrine and assured that Aristotelianism would not undermine Catholic theology.

Bacon's and Descartes' viewpoints on natural philosophy became objects of national pride. English intellectuals praised the former and French intellectuals lauded the latter. Salesmanship entered the picture too. What little reason occurred in Bacon's empiricist view was marketed by him and his supporters as a new type of reason termed inductive reason. They contrasted it with the existing type, called deductive reason, which made up Descartes rationalism and had been elaborated by Aristotle. Inductive reason and its basis, inductive logic, were promoted by Englishmen as indispensable to improving natural philosophy. Not until the early 1700s did national pride subside enough to allow Europeans to generally agree on the roles observation and reason play in learning about nature. And not until this happened could a reformed natural philosophy take shape in Europe.

A thing Bacon's and Descartes' viewpoints had in common was a belief that only one of the four kinds of causation, causality, or cause identified by Aristotle is worth considering when learning about nature; namely, efficient causation and thus efficient causes, effects, and cause-effect relationships (causal relationships). Efficient causation would also be increasingly referred to as determinism after approximately 1875. This was accompanied by a tendency to replace cause, effect, and causal relationship with the term's antecedent, consequent, and deterministic relationship, largely by physicists and individuals seeing physics as the model science.

The two men were at odds in regard to atomism. Atomism is the idea that everything in nature — the universe — is due to the incessan drifting together and then apart of countless, minuscule, hard, indestructible, eternal, indivisible, perpetually-moving particles of matter. These particles are called atoms. Bacon accepted atomism but

Descartes rejected it. In accepting atomism Bacon was part of a rising tide of natural philosophers who in attempting to reform natural philosophy entertained ancient ideas Aristotle either overlooked or felt were wrong. One idea Aristotle felt was wrong is atomism. For it implies there exists between atoms an emptiness, nothingness, void, or vacuum, which he claimed is impossible. From his claim we get the expression 'nature abhors a vacuum'. Aristotle and Descartes believed nature is a continuous substance, a plenum, which while varying in density never becomes spread so thin that it stops existing and thereby gives way to a nothingness. The atomism Descartes rejected and that Bacon, along with a growing number of modern natural philosophers, accepted was an idea championed by the ancient Greek philosopher Democritos, who had lived roughly a century before Aristotle.

The crucial step in reforming natural philosophy was made about 1685 by the Englishman Isaac Newton when he took an intermediate stance on the observation-reason issue that would be slowly accepted by most of Europe's natural philosophers as the 1700s progressed. Although Bacon hadn't said deductive reason is totally worthless in generating knowledge about nature, he did minimize its value. Newton, however, felt deductive reason was potentially of greater value in generating this knowledge than was inductive reason. But for deductive reason to actually be of greater value it had to be altered. Newton performed the necessary alteration. His alteration was to stipulate that the conclusion implied by true premises in a valid deductive argument (a deductive argument exhibiting validity) is not to be thought true, as was typically done, until what this conclusion says is subsequently borne out by observation. Such a conclusion he called an hypothesis to underscore the tentativeness of its truth; meaning either no observations pertaining to it have been made or only a few such observations have been made, all of which show it is probably true.

Unfortunately, Newton's belief that both reason (in the form of hypotheses implied by premises in valid deductive arguments) and observation are equally important didn't become quickly known. The reason why is that it was not set forth in a paper devoted just to it. Instead, his belief was nestled within a treatise he wrote around 1685 in which he utilized it to come up with an hypothesis to explain how gravitation (the force caused by gravity) accounts for, or explains, the motions of all things in the universe. This was Newton's hypothesis of universal gravitation. About 1710, the hypothesis was renamed Newton's theory of universal gravitation, theory connoting an elevation in its truth status warranted by many observations having been made over the preceding 25 years attesting to the hypothesis' probable truth. Not until around 1735 did natural philosophers begin to discover, ponder, understand, admire, and want to employ the hypothetico-deductive method (the method of deducing hypotheses from premises) Newton used to generate his initially hypothetical, subsequently theoretical knowledge about all motion. And not until the mid 1800s would they commence honing his method into what about 1875 came to be the scientific method we know today (page 3). Three things may be said of Newton. First, he accepted determinism/ efficient causation. Second, the universality of efficient causation implied by his theory of universal gravitation led to determinism being sometimes dubbed Newtonian determinism. Third, he embraced atomism and therefore was an atomist.

While the relationship between observation and reason was perhaps the key detail on which agreement was needed in order for a reformed natural philosophy to manifest itself, it was not the only detail. Opinions vary as to what the remaining ones were and how well consensus on them was reached among *concerned* natural philosophers. The italics here signify that a majority of natural philosophers were content to work on their research and theories and weren't all that concerned about such abstract matters, just like the majority of today's scientists could care less about the abstract goings-on within the philosophy of science. At any rate, sufficient consensus was obviously reached on these other details, since by 1800 a reformed natural philosophy existed in Europe. This isn't to say the 1800s and 1900s saw harmony everywhere within science. In those centuries details bearing on the fundamentals of one science or another were debated, often hotly, by factions in that science, as happened in biology between the reductionists (mechanists or molecular biologists) and the vitalists and in psychology between the behaviorists and the gestaltists. Yet these debates within a science rarely spilled over into another science and never into science overall, where they might precipitate a crisis in the foundation of science, a so-called foundation crisis. That such debates have taken place is not to be interpreted as a weakness in science but, to the contrary, as a sign of science's strength. They are healthy signs, signs that science is mature and secure enough to allow and even foster debates. Also they indicate science is a democratic social institution, though, as with any social institution, bowing to authority is expected.

What agreement besides the need for both observation and reason was reached on other details? Again, opinions on this vary. Mine are:

1. Explanations must be based on efficient causation (determinism) and must not be based on the other three kinds of causation Aristotle identified, which were final causation, formal causation, and material causation. Explanations based on efficient causation are referred to as causal or deterministic explanations. Special attention should be paid to assuring that final causation and formal causation are not even hinted at, due to their popularity between 1200 and 1600 having severely limited the generation of worthwhile knowledge about nature. Final causation explains a thing by specifying the final cause, or purpose, of that thing. Closely associated with final causation is teleology, the study of purpose. Explanations based on purpose/final causation are called teleological explanations.

2. All things in nature, or the universe, must be regarded as being due to and composed of matter and/or energy derived from matter, an idea termed materialism. Special attention should be paid to assuring that nature isn't seen as possessing forces of a nonmaterial sort, nonmaterial forces being implied by such words as mystical, occult, esoteric, magical, and arcane. Intuition as a basis for knowing nature must be avoided since it and consequently its knowledge (intuitive knowledge, popularly called mystical knowledge) imply the existence of nonmaterial forces. Historically, intuiting nature resulted in several notable mystical philosophies. Probably the first was that of the ancient Greek philosopher Pythagoras, whose philosophy - Pythagoreanism- influenced the ancient Greek philosopher Plato, who taught Aristotle. Plato's semi-mystical philosophy, Platonic philosophy or Platonism, was gradually made, from 250 to 1450, more mystical in the guise of neoplatonic philosophy, or neoPlatonism. Now the appeals of Platonism, neo-Platonism, Pythagoreanism, and Hermeticism during renaissance and early modern times was of grave concern to reformers of natural philosophy. So one of their aims was to rid natural philosophy, especially chemistry and biology, of anything mystical/intuitive and to then immunize it against future occult encroachment.

3. Matter is to be viewed as composed of nothing but atoms, which are as small as matter/material things can get. Specifics regarding the characteristics of atoms need not be those stated by Democritos. As an aside, ancient Greek atomism evolved into a theory about atoms — an atomic theory — about 1810.

4. It is logically possible (possible 'in principle' or possible 'in theory") to explain anything in nature in terms of the atoms comprising it. Put another way, it is (logically) possible to reduce anything in nature to its constituent atoms. Hence the name given this idea, reductionism. Implicit to reductionism is that such reductionistic explanations are not only possible but desirable. Therefore, time spent developing causal explanations should be spent developing causal reductionistic explanations, unless/until doing so isn't/is no longer empirically possible. Nature is a hierarchy of things (atoms) within things (molecules) within things (eg., organelles) within things (e.g., cells) within things (e.g., tissues) within things (e.g., organs) within things (eg., bodily systems) within things (e.g., fish) within things (e.g., groups such as schools of fish), etc., all the way up through planets, stars, solar systems, galaxies to the universe itself. Believers in reductionism, termed reductionists, do not say we must reduce — analyze — a thing we want to explain (e.g., a fish) down to the atoms comprising it. But they do say reduction - analysis - should be down to the lowest level of organization which provides a satisfying explanation of the thing of interest. Here again we see reformers of natural philosophy doing their utmost to eliminate all need to resort to acknowledging the existence of nonmaterial things, like the life force promoted by vitalists in biology from 1700 to 1850 and the formative/holistic principle advocated by neovitalists in biology and gestaltists in psychology between 1900 and 1950.

5. Finally, explanations must be created from descriptions of relationships between characteristics/properties/attributes of things. The gist of what's meant by said relationships may be illustrated thusly. Consider two things, a ball and a ramp. Also consider two characteristics, a characteristic of the ball and a characteristic of the ramp. Assume that the characteristic of the ball is its speed and that the characteristic of the ramp is its slope, or angle. Further assume the situation examined is this ball rolling down this ramp.

The relationship between the two characteristics would be the coinciding of degrees of ball speed with degrees of ramp slope. And the gist of what is meant by descriptions of relationships is this. The description of the relationship between (ball) speed and (ramp) slope states how changes in speed coincide with- relate to- changes in slope or, in other words, how changes in speed are related to changes in slope. A description may be verbal (use words), graphic (use a graph), or analytic (use an equation). Only a rough description is possible with words, which is why scientists avoid verbal descriptions where possible. Graphic descriptions are pleasing to the eye, yet often difficult to utilize (it can be hard pinpointing the quantities they depict). Analytic descriptions are the most useful of all. However, they are meaningless to people who lack the skill to make sense out of them. Although we say we 'observe' the characteristics of things, characteristics are actually conceptualizations, conceptions, or concepts and therefore products of our imagination! Now concepts, be they of characteristics or other ideas, can be imagined to lie along a dimension that stretches from very concrete (e.g., color, weight, slope, speed, pressure) to very abstract (e.g., speciation, motivation, electricity, gravitation, causation). Beginning in the late 1500s, the Italian physicist and astronomer Galileo Galilei, Galileo for short, precisely described with mathematics many relationships between characteristics involving moving bodies, movements, or motion (e.g., balls rolling down ramps), the study of which is an old branch of physics referred to as mechanics. Some natural philosophers during the 1600s and 1700s felt Galileo's approach to knowing nature (i.e., via measurements and equations) ought to be a component of the research aspect of the method employed by a reformed natural philosophy. The essence of his approach survives in the research being done today.

We can see in most of these details an attempt to transform the natural philosophy which existed before 1600 into something impervious to purpose, nonmaterial forces, and intuition. Also we can see why modern science and modern religion have had a relationship that has been awkward and strained. Their relationship has been made tense, too, by modern science being seen by some people as being at odds with religion and even trying to destroy it.

Emergence of a reformed natural philosophy which around 1875 would start being termed modern science was facilitated by technological and mathematical developments that natural philosophers found they could make into powerful means for attaining their end of knowing nature. The timing of these developments was perfect! For had they not occurred when they did, the reformation in natural philosophy wouldn't have gotten anywhere near as far as it did. We will end this chapter with a summary of the more salient of these developments in technology and mathematics, developments which have given science many of its tools of the trade and have equipped the scientific method with many of its techniques.

Technological developments beneficial to modern science included the microscope (1590), telescope (circa 1608), thermometer (circa 1620), barometer (1643), galvanometer (1821), microtome (circa 1825), thermopile (1830), kymograph (1847), spectroscope (1861), seismograph (1880), oscillograph (1897), centrifuge (circa 1900), chromatograph (1906), cloud chamber (1911), X-ray diffraction techniques (1912), radioactive isotope tracers (1923), Warburg manometer/apparatus (1923), ultracentrifuge (1923), electroencephalograph (1929), cyclotron (1930), radio telescope (1937), electron microscope (1939), electronic computer (1944), carbon-14 dating (1947), and increasingly more accurate clocks and balances (weighing scales). Mathematical developments benefiting modern science included the invention of the symbolic algebra we know today (over the period 1550 to 1650), analytic geometry (1637), probability theory (circa 1655), calculus (circa 1685), non-Euclidean geometries (beginning around 1800), and statistics (circa 1835). Still another development which benefited modern science was creation of the metric system in France in 1795. It standardized the units of measurement of various characteristics (e.g., length, area, volume, and weight). This allowed scientists everywhere to speak the same language when it comes to comparing measurements they make of the characteristics of things they study.

References*

Butterfield, Herbert <u>The Origins of Modern Science</u>. New York: The Free Press, 1965 (revised edition) (fairly easy). Note that, while an old book, this still paints in about 250 pages a good picture of not only natural philosophy between 1300 and 1800 but the social and religious climates influencing it.

Jevons, W. Stanley <u>The Principles Of Science: A Treatise On Logic And Scientific Method</u>. New York: Dover, 1958 (hard). This is an unabridged, unaltered republication of the second edition, originally published in 1877. Only readers wanting a good feel for the congealing thoughts in the mid 1870s on what the scientific method is will find tackling this fine book's 770 pages worth the effort.

Kline, Morris <u>Mathematics And The Search For Knowledge</u>. New York: Oxford University Press, 1985 (fairly easy). A well thought out synopsis of how science has utilized mathematics, primarily from renaissance times onward.

Lindberg, David C. <u>The Beginnings Of Western Science</u>. Chicago: The University of Chicago Press, 1992 (fairly easy). Covers the period 600 B.C. to 1450.

Madden, Edward H. (Editor) <u>Theories of Scientific method: The Renaissance through the Nineteenth Century.</u> New York: Gordon and Breach, 1989 (fairly hard) Detailed summaries of thoughts on the scientific method by such notables as Francis Bacon (1561-1626), Rene Descartes (1596-1650), Isaac Newton (1642-1727), John Herschel (1738-1822), William Whewell (1794-1866), John Stuart Mill (1806-1873), W. Stanley Jevons (1835-1892), and Charles S. Peirce (1839-1914),

Teresi, Dick <u>Lost Discoveries</u>. New York: Simon & Schuster, 2000 (easy). This is an excellent supplement to Lindberg's book. It delves into aspects of ancient and medieval science that fall largely outside of the so-called western tradition in science, which mainly traces the history of science from ancient Greece to the medieval Islamic Empire to renaissance Europe to finally modern Europe.

----

*References at the end of a chapter in this book are sources for readers to consult to learn more about the topics discussed or are sources I cited in the chapter. They aren't all the sources I consulted in writing that chapter. References intended as sources for readers to consult have within parentheses after them my feeling of their level of difficulty for the averagely intelligent person (easy, fairly easy, fairly hard, and hard).

CHAPTER 2

Science's Empirical Side

The last chapter said science has two sides, one empirical (observation) and the other rational (reason). It also might have been taken to imply these. Two sides are linked to thetwo aspects — research and theory — of the scientific method, suggesting that the empirical side pertains only to research and the rational side only to theory. But implying such a linkage was not my intent. For both sides of science manifest themselves in both aspects of science's method, albeit in different proportions and ways. Thus, reason enters into doing research and observation enters into creating theories. Reason, for instance, guides wording and relating the propositions (statements) making up theories, designing research studies, troubleshooting problems encountered while conducting studies, noting questionable interpretations of analyses of data collected in studies, and identifying fraudulent research practices.

Every reader has pieced together a personal knowledge about nature. Most readers think they understand how they have done this. Hence they will feel it not necessary and even an insult to their intelligence to learn we are going to start this chapter by examining the nitty gritty of how they have come to personally know nature. I feel this preliminary examination is needed. For there are mental processes largely unknown to most people that determine how we individually come to know nature. Understanding them will help us to better understand how we collectively come to know nature and, by extension, how scientists get to know it. So please bear with me.

As our birth draws near, we grow more aware- conscious- of the things happening outside us. Roughly two months after being born, awareness of these things escalates as our senses rapidly mature. A year after birth we are distinguishing ourselves from our environment, an environment whose countless things include other selves. By four years old we think of the things we sense as being similar or dissimilar in particular ways. We also start organizing our thoughts about things into groups. Some of these groups consist of things such as me, mother, brother, food, bed, room, people, house, yard, flower, tree, etc. Other groups address the ways in which things are similar or dissimilar: their color, size, shape, loudness, hardness, weight, temperature, movement, kindness, etc. At four years old we are largely not conscious/aware of the groups we are creating in our mind and do not realize that they are continually shaping our awareness of all the things we observe, thereby imbuing them with meaning. In fact, at fifty years old we are still largely unaware/unconscious of these mental matters. Upon becoming adults, we may learn that psychologists say this is how our mind operates and that mental groups are known as concepts. We may learn too that concepts about similarities/dissimilarities between things are what scientists refer to as the characteristics (properties or attributes) of things and that scientists often refer to the characteristics of a thing as variables when they study it.

When we start organizing thoughts about things into concepts or, put in other words, start forming concepts about them and their characteristics, we pretty much stop sensing things and begin perceiving them. Perceiving (perception) is a blend of sensing (sensation), remembering (memory), and motivation. Hence perception and its end result, percepts, are more than simply sensation and its end result, sensations. Although we as adults continue to say we see, hear, touch, smell, taste, etc. things we should realize that nearly always these words really designate percepts and not sensations. Which means the word observation normally signifies perception, not sensation. Perception is the basis for conceiving (concept formation) and its and result, concepts.

Several things are noteworthy about concepts. First, they are personal. My concept Father — my father — is similar to yet not the same as yours. Second, once formed, my concept of a thing (eg., a river) or characteristic of things (e.g., their hardness) tends to change with the passage of time. For example, my concept automobile is today not quite the same as twenty years ago, even a week ago (if, say, yesterday I was in auto accident). Third, a concept is a reference point against which observations are compared to ascertain whether they resemble the concept well enough to be regarded instances of it. In this respect a concept is very much like an electronic pattern recognizer, a device for recognizing a certain, say, light or sound pattern by determining whether the patterns it *observes* are or are not the same as its reference pattern.

Fourth, the personal concepts we've been discussing are not verbalized because there are no words for them. They exist in our heads as unnamed impressions. Now in order for what is in my head to get into your head I must communicate with you. If we rule out extrasensory communication (telepathy), then my communicating with you must be through sensory communication. Sensory communication or, simply, communication typically employs words in spoken or written form. Words stand for impersonal concepts a society has created out of the personal concepts of its members so that members can communicate with each other. Therefore, we have unverbalized personal concepts and verbalized impersonal concepts. In order for me to communicate with you, I must know impersonal concepts well enough to pick the one that best reflects in its verbalized meaning- its dictionary definition- the unverbalized meaning of the personal concept of mine that I wish to tell you.

Learning language is learning the vocabulary and grammar needed to communicate with others. Vocabulary is the words needed, all of them designating impersonal concepts. Grammar is the rules needed for organizing words into sentences and sentences into paragraphs so as to verbalize relationships among impersonal concepts that reflect relationships among personal concepts. Suppose you speak or write to me about your job. This entails you linking your unverbalized personal concepts to those verbalized impersonal concepts which best convey their meaning, followed by me attaching these verbalized impersonal concepts to those personal concepts within my concept repertoire whose meaning is most like their meaning. Communications engineers characterize this process as you encoding a message (signal) followed by me decoding it.

A final remark on concepts is they influence our observation of things and thereby our impression of reality. This they do by predisposing us to interpret things we observe as being or not being examples of them. Now to the extent a thing we observe is thought to be an instance of a concept then to that extent the thing is given meaning by the concept and therefore becomes meaningful to us. To the extent this does not happen, then to that extent the thing will lack meaning and be meaningless to us. After things become meaningful to us, they largely lose their identity by merging with the concept they resemble, which slightly changes the concept's meaning. By things largely losing their identity can perhaps be clarified by likening them to a light bulb which usually is off and under only rare conditions is on, as when an emergency backup light in a house automatically turns on during a power failure. The upshot of all this is that our personal knowledge generally exists as conceptualized empirical knowledge whose facets are mainly concepts and relationships between concepts and whose concepts influence and are influenced by our future observations.

This discussion of concepts is intended to lessen the tendency of some to believe that observing things and their characteristics results in a knowledge about nature which is a 100% accurate portrait of nature. However, my saying so should not be taken as me in effect saying observation can't generate useful knowledge about nature. That this isn't true is seen in all the knowledge science has amassed over the last four centuries. My point here in observation has limits and its limits restrict the accuracy of both personal knowledge and scientific knowledge. Having made these remarks, we continue our discussion of personal knowledge.

`Many things occur during our first four years of life. They serve as a foundation on which future thoughts and actions take place. From birth to two years old we do what science basically does: observe things in our environment. Sometimes we do no more than observe a thing (passive observation). Other times we observe and manipulate a thing (active observation). With active observation, we learn about reactions of things to our actions. From this arises a personal concept which takes the form of a principle (generalization). It is the principle of causality, causation, or cause (our actions) and effect (a thing's reactions to our actions). Its applied version is the means-ends principle, our utilizing certain things (termed means) to obtain other things (termed ends). As we observe we notice that some things happen together, from which sprout the principles of regularity and predictability. Now if two or more things always occur together, then a scientist says they display lawfulness or are related to each other in a lawful fashion or constitute a lawful relationship (a law).

By seven years old we're fairly adept at thinking about things in terms of where and when they occur. We have also begun to conceive their where and when as two out of the various characteristics of all things, place and time. Eventually we may substitute the word space for the word place and then think of things as having space and time as two of their characteristics. Science treats space and time as being the contextual characteristics of all things, the contexts within which things occur. More precisely, it envisions things happening at certain points — locations — in space (their where) and time (their when) and occupying certain amounts of space (their length, width, height, area, volume, etc.) and time (their duration).

At age seven, thoughts about things and their characteristics start to get complicated. We pay increasing attention to the spatial (space) relationships between things, temporal (time) relationships between them, and spatiotemporal (space-time) relationships between them. Also our thoughts go beyond things (e.g., your mother or my mother) to groups of things (a group of mothers, or mother) and their characteristics (e.g., their size, actions, beliefs, etc.). Now it is commonly said we observe things, relationships between things, groups (of things), relationships between groups, characteristics (of things/groups), and relationships between characteristics (of things/groups). And it would be awkward to say otherwise. Yet, strictly speaking, we only observe things. Never do we observe a relationship between things, a group, a relationship between groups, a characteristic, or a relationship between characteristics. Instead we construct, invent, or imagine them to exist, maybe by employing a blend of observation, reason, and intuition. Consequently, our knowledge of them is in the form of mental constructs (figments of our imagination). This is so for both personal knowledge and scientific knowledge.

After turning ten years old, we are inclined to think hypothetically. Hypothetical thinking entails four steps. First, by exercising our imagination we come up with a relationship of interest we think could exist. Therefore a relationship is hypothesized or, equivalently, an hypothesis is created. Second, we think of what we could observe that would, if observed, indicate the hypothesis is probably true and hence the relationship probably exists. This step is the deducing of a sub-hypothesis implied (predicted) by the hypothesis created in the first step. Third, we observe what we picked in the second step as indicating the relationship exists. Fourth, we decide from what is observed that the relationship (first step) probably does or does not exist. If we conclude it doesn't exist, then we may decide to next slightly modify the relationship and repeat the last three steps to find out whether this modified relationship exists.

Several comments are desirable. One is that hypothetical thinking is the interplay between observation and reason which characterizes the hypothetico-deductive method conceived by Newton (page 8). The second step is rational and the third is empirical. Another remark is that observation in the third step can be either passive or active. Still another is that passive and active observation may be either unsystematic or systematic. Research relies on systematic (orderly) observation! Lastly, passive systematic observation is called naturalistic observation and active systematic observation is known as controlled observation. Research studies employing naturalistic observation are known as naturalistic studies; research studies utilizing controlled observation are referred to as experimental studies, or experiments. These distinctions are made in all research, be it scientific or nonscientific.

It should be pointed out that experiment has two other meanings. One is within the context of probability theory, in which an experiment is the process of observing things and/or the observations that are the result of this process. The other is the 'thought experiment', a deductive kind of argument which resembles a child playing a game of make-believe or what if. While a thought experiment is inspired by past observations that suggest the existence of an interesting relationship and may inspire future observations, it does not itself involve making observations. Scientists occasionally conduct thought experiments, even though they do not always call them that. The better-known thought experiments are those performed by theoretically inclined and thus theoretical physicists, Galileo and Albert Einstein being well known for theirs. In a thought experiment a scientist deduces a conclusion implied/predicted by premises he imagines to be true (his what ifs).

We now move from personal knowledge to scientific knowledge, concentrating on its empirical side. Although scientific knowledge resembles personal knowledge, the two aren't the same. The key differences between them are as follow. Personal knowledge is acquired by one person during his or her lifetime. Scientific knowledge is accumulated by numerous scientists over the course of many centuries. All of the items making up scientific knowledge are referred to as generalizations (principles). Science considers them tentative, indicating they could change — maybe a lot — in light of future research. At any moment science has a prevailing, or accepted, viewpoint on this or that aspect of nature (the universe): earthquakes, cancer, black holes, mental illness, the atmosphere, biological or geological or cosmic (the universe's) evolution, galaxies, economic stability, UFOs, etc. Some scientists forget, or ignore, the tentativeness of scientific knowledge/generalizations/principles and continue to accept something that research has shown to not likely be true, which prompts other scientists to see them as being dogmatic (close-minded).

Exactly what does science endeavor to know about nature? The goal of science is to acquire an explanatory knowledge of things in nature (i.e., explanations of them in terms of their efficient causes, or simply their causes). Before science can have this explanatory knowledge, it needs a descriptive knowledge of things (i.e., descriptions of them in terms of their characteristics). And before science can have this descriptive knowledge, it needs an existential knowledge of things (i.e., it needs to know they exist). Different sciences have moved at different rates obtaining an existential followed by a descriptive followed by an explanatory knowledge of things. Today, the social sciences are still busy accruing descriptive knowledge while the natural sciences are largely preoccupied with creating explanatory knowledge.

Scientific explanations of nature differ from nonscientific ones by being rigorous, abstract, and general. Rigorous means they are inspired by reliable scientific descriptions. Abstract means they abstract (i.e., analyze, dissect, or remove) from things of interest their characteristics of interest and then proceed to describe a relationship between these characteristics. This is made possible by conceptualizing characteristics (making them into concepts). General, here, means scientific explanations apply to all, not some, things of a certain type (e.g., stars and crows).

All things of a specific kind are called members of the population of all such things; *some things* of a specific kind are called members of a sample of all these things. Usually it is impossible or unfeasible to observe a *population* of things. In such cases a fairly small number of members in the population is selected to also be members of a *sample*. This is done in a way that assures the sample will mirror, reflect, or represent the population. For only then can we justifiably conclude that what was learned by observing the sample is essentially the same as what would have been learned had it been possible/feasible for us to observe the population. The population from which a sample is drawn, (created) is termed the population sampled and the process of drawing (creating) a sample is called sampling. It is assumed a sample can never be a perfect mirror image of its population. And to the extent a sample isn't a perfect representative of its population is attributed to sampling error (i.e., errors in creating the sample).

Science explains the differences between things of a certain type/population in terms of relationships between their characteristics and, sometimes, in terms of differences between two or more types/populations of things. Put more succinctly, science explains the relationships between two or more characteristics of things. Herein lies the reason for science devoting most of its time to studying relationships between characteristics. Once a relationship between characteristics is described, the description may be employed to explain the relationship. And after three relationships between characteristics have been described, science can, if fortunate, utilize one of these relationships to explain the other two. This is accomplished by making the two relationships to be explained the premises in a deductive argument and making the third, their explanation, the conclusion in that argument.

Explanation can be viewed as either an answer to the question how or an answer to the question why such-and-such happened. Is there a difference between the two questions? Scientists think there is. To them the question why asks for a teleological explanation, explanation in terms of final causation/purpose. Recall that item 1 on the top of page 9 said the reformers of natural philosophy didn't want to have anything to do with final causation/purpose. Like those reformers, contemporary scientists feel the question how reflects both their commitment to explanations based on efficient causation/determinism and their desire to study causal/deterministic relationships. Parenthetically, notice that the word because indicates the words following it constitute our causal explanation of something.

Relationships between characteristics are classified according to how often they have been observed (by at least a few people) and hence according to the probable truth they actually exist. A relationship not yet observed or observed only a very few times is termed an hypothetical relationship or hypothesis. Claims it exists are respectively treated as unconfirmed or poorly confirmed and therefore, at best, as maybe true. A relationship observed a dozen or so times is called a theoretical relationship or theory. Claims it exists are treated as fairly well confirmed and probably true. A relationship observed a few dozen times is termed a lawful relationship or law. Now hypotheses, theories, and laws explain. Thus the terms hypothetical explanation, theoretical explanation, and lawful explanation. In the next chapter we look at how observation is employed to confirm relationships. We'll also discuss boundary conditions, conditions specifying boundaries, or limits, within which a relationship can be reasonably expected to hold (to exist). Boundary conditions need to be taken into account when judging the likely truth of statements saying that relationships exist.

Hypotheses, theories, and laws are typically named after the key characteristic they address. Earlier we said that around 1685 Newton introduced his hypothesis of universal gravitation. It is named after its key characteristic, gravitation. This hypothesis also nicely illustrates how a relationship's truth status can progress with the accumulation of evidence - observations - confirming its existence. About 1710 Newton's hypothesis of universal gravitation evolved into his theory of universal gravitation. Then, in the late 1700s, Newton's theory commenced being increasingly dignified as his law of universal gravitation. Although typically thought by many to be an eternal truth, this law ought to still be viewed as tentative. For it might no longer be true if the universe were to change significantly.

Determinism originally meant that the state of one characteristic in a relationship is exactly, strictly, or rigorously determined by the state(s) of the relationship's other characteristic(s). Exactitude had to be qualified in the early 1900s. That is when the new quantum theory of physics forced physicists to admit there is a far less exact determinism operating at the atomic level of matter. The two kinds of determinism were reconciled after a boundary condition (the size of things) was placed on exact determinism, which restricted its applicability. Whereupon exact determinism was viewed as emerging out of the inexact determinism applicable to atoms. Exact determinism is traditionally known as Newtonian determinism; inexact determinism is normally called statistical determinism.

Be careful not to read too much into the statistical of statistical determinism. Statistical determinism would have perhaps been better called probabilistic determinism, since details about it are clarified more frequently with techniques of probability theory than with those of statistics. The important thing to know is that statistical analyses done in research conducted in psychology, sociology, education, business, etc. are not done because members of the typically human populations studied are thought to be governed by statistical determinism. Rather, they are done because they are usually how knowledge about populations is generated (e.g., about the relationship between the characteristics reading achievement, verbal aptitude, and achievement motivation in all eighth graders). Does this therefore imply humans are under the influence of Newtonian determinism? The question opens a can of worms, the determinism (no free-will) versus indeterminism (free-will) issue in philosophy.

Despite the commonsensical truth and feeling of reassurance offered by the adage 'seeing is believing', the empirical roots of science and everyday life are not all that substantial. For as indicated on page 19, we observe things but not relationships between things, groups, relationships between groups, characteristics, and relationships between characteristics. Nor are the material roots of science and everyday life as secure as was once thought, given the apparent nonmateriality of subatomic particles making up atoms. The physicist Robert Jastrow drew an analogy between atoms and the Astrodome (now gone) in Houston, Texas:

> "If (the diameter of) the outer shell of electrons in the atom were the size of the Astrodome that covers the Houston basball stadium, the nucleus (protons and neutrons) would be a Ping pong ball in the center of the stadium. That is the emptiness of the atom." (Jastrow, 1967, p 9)

Notice my referring before the above quotation to the apparent nonmateriality of subatomic particles. Whether or not protons, electrons, and neutrons are composed of matter is up for grabs. Measurements of them can just as easily be in units of mass (how much matter they contain) as in units of energy (how much energy they release). If we think of subatomic particles being simultaneously matter and energy, then their energy can be viewed as material energy (i.e., energy derived from matter). This would imply that subatomic particles only appear nonmaterial and that 99.9% of the volume in space occupied by an atom is bathed in material energy, not nonmaterial energy (i.e., energy emanating from a nonmaterial thing).

The philosopher of science Norwood Hanson delved into the way concepts affect how we observe things. He was fascinated with visual illusions studied by gestalt psychologists in the early 1900s. One of his insights is worth mentioning. Hanson said we do not 'see'. Instead, we 'see as if. By this he meant that, rather than seeing a thing in all its individuality and uniqueness, we see a thing as if it is the concept that seeing it brought to mind. Our propensity to conceptualize creates, though we are rarely aware of it, a bias (meaning a systematic, as opposed to random, error) in our observation of nature which distorts our picture of nature. This is what Hanson meant when he said that our knowledge, personal and scientific, about nature is theory-laden. Perhaps a better term would be concept-laden, or even concept-driven.

Concept-laden empirical knowledge and the truism appearances can be deceiving are illustrated by thinking about what we've in fact observed as we have seen throughout our lives (on clear days) the sun rise and set, rise and set, rise and set, etc. day in and day out. What is implied by these observations? The answer depends upon reasoning what happens at night, between sunset and sunrise. Reason may indicate that sometime during the night the sun stops moving west and starts moving east, underneath where we live (on the "side" of earth opposite our side), until it rises again in the east. Assume this That is what reason implies. By making what is observed in the daytime and what's reasoned about at nighttime two premises in a deductive-type argument we are able to deduce the following conclusion: alternating days and nights are determined, caused by the sun going around the earth or, as astronomers would say, revolving in an orbit around the earth and thus orbiting earth. This is one possible explanation, or theory, of the alternation between day and night. It is the geocentric explanation/theory widely accepted until roughly 1650. Specifically, it was Aristotle's and Ptolemy's astronomical theories that were mentioned on page 4. The theory/explanation gets its name from it making earth (geo) the center (centric) of the universe, the hub round which the sun and all the other celestial bodies revolve.

In the mid 1600s, Europeans began replacing Aristotle's and Ptolemy's geocentric theories with a heliocentric theory set forth by Nicholas Copernicus a century earlier. According to it, our sun is the hub round which earth and all other planets revolve in a solar, or sun-centered, system. It said earth rotates (spins) and that its rotation is what causes alternating days and nights. Now switching from one view to the other led to a new way of seeing ourselves. Geocentrism had long sustained an egocentrism, or self-centeredness, and anthropocentrisen (human-centeredness) that led us to see ourselves as being something special because we live in a special place within the universe, at its center. People feeling their uniqueness threatened by heliocentrism held onto geocentrism by reminding themselves of the adage 'seeing is believing. By 1700, most well-educated people knew and accepted heliocentrism.

Observing nature with the intent of painting an accurate picture of it is challenging. To have any chance at success, we must observe nature systematically. This has been known since the beginning of Sumerian times, around 3500 B.C. Systematic observation pays close attention to details, carefully records what's observed (on clay tablets, papyrus scrolls, notepads, data sheets, questionnaires, tape recorders, etc.), is planned ahead of time, and specifies all conditions known or suspected to influence what will be observed (the relevant conditions of a research study) so one person can replicate — repeat — the procedure another person employed in order to evaluate that person's observations/findings. Observations may be unaided (e.g., using simply our eyes or ears) or aided by things like rulers, clocks, scales, thermometers, microscopes, telescopes, spectroscopes, voltmeters, seismographs, MRI (magnetic resonance imaging), visual acuity tests, and psychological tests. They are called data if either simple or relatively unorganized and called information if either complex or relatively organized. Also they are sometimes termed facts. Observations viewed as data are typically measurements (e.g., 18 inches) and hence numbers (eg., 18) followed by a unit of measurement (e.g., the inch). Data in the form of measurements are more specifically called tallies, counts, readings, meter readings, pointer readings, readouts, scores, etc.

Nearly all systematic observation performed by scientists before around 1600 was naturalistic observation (page 20). Which means nearly all scientific research prior to that time was naturalistic research. Such research exerts relatively little control over relevant conditions. The usual reason for this is that things affecting the things observed (e.g., stars, tsunamis, and prehistoric artifacts) are beyond our control. But occasionally the reason is that while control is possible it is not desirable because it will interrupt the natural unfolding of events the researcher seeks to know (eg, soil erosion, dominance relationships among elk, and conflict resolution between children). Control of relevant conditions may be physical and/or statistical. Physical control is of two types, selection and manipulation. Naturalistic research employs control by selection: selecting, say, the things to observe or the conditions under which they are observed. Starting about 1925, naturalistic research sometimes supplemented control by selection with statistical control (control by means of statistical techniques).

Around 1600, systematic observation done by some scientists, mainly physicists, began to be more active. Active systematic observation is called controlled observation. Research studies utilizing it are called experimental studies experiments.Experimental research exerts relatively much control over relevant conditions. Basically, it is naturalistic research to which control by manipulation is added. Manipulation may be in the form of a characteristic (e.g., temperature) of a thing (e.g., a room) being made to exist in only one of its possible states (e.g., 70 degrees Fahrenheit) during the time that observations are performed, thereby holding (keeping) the characteristic constant (making it into a constant). Also manipulation can take the form of a characteristic being made to exist in each of two or more of its possible states (e.g., 65, 70, and 75 degrees) when observations take place, thus varying the characteristic (making it into a variable). The characteristic in question may be either a systematic variable or a random variable. A variable can be manipulated into being systematic or be selected for already being that way. Whichever, a systematic variable is a characteristic whose possible states occur in a systematic (nonrandom) manner. A random variable is a characteristic whose possible. states occur in a random (unsystematic) fashion. By about 1650, experimental research had become a noticeable percentage of all scientific research done.

Controlling relevant conditions is relative, not absolute. Seldom is it 0% and never is it 100%. Nor is there a clear line separating naturalistic observation (naturalistic research) from controlled observation (experimental research). Instead, there's a sizable grey area, which in the mid 1960s commenced being referred to as quasi-experimental research. Good examples of such research are the field experiments performed by certain biologists and sociologists and by certain nonscientists (e.g., education researchers). Note that the observatories of astronomers and the laboratories of physicists, chemists, biologists, and psychologists are designed, built and equipped to foster accurate naturalistic observation and accurate controlled observation, respectively. Also note that the blinds constructed by field biologists permit them to observe, naturalistically and thus unobtrusively, the activities of wildlife.

Controversy has surrounded the merits of naturalistic versus experimental research when it comes to discovering and describing causal relationships. Most experts on the subject think naturalistic research usually lacks the caliber of control needed to discern the subtleties distinguishing causal from noncausal (acausal) relationships. There are a few who claim that even experimental research is ill suited to this, which is why they advocate searching for noncausal rather than causal relationships. Physicists who study subatomic particles especially feel this way, given their inability so far to find strictly deterministic relationships.

References

Brown, Harold I. <u>Perception, Theory and Commitment. The New Philosophy of Science</u>. Chicago: University of Chicago Press, 1977 (hard). Excellent discussion of the problems with the philosophy of science known as logical positivism and of solutions to them proposed between about 1957 and 1972, solutions offered by Karl Popper (falsification of hypotheses), Norwood Hanson (theory-laden observation/knowledge), Michael Scriven (problems with deductive-type explanations), Thomas Kuhn (nature of scientific revolutions), Michael Polanyi (personal knowledge), and Nelson Goodman (confirmation of hypotheses).

Harré, Rom <u>Great Scientific Experiments</u>. Oxford (England): Phaidon Press, 1981. (fairly easy). Insight into the kinds of thinking entering into scientific research of the experimental sort, as disclosed by looking at twenty experiments, mostly done after 1600, conducted for different reasons and occurring within different social contexts.

Jastrow, Robert <u>Red Giants And White Dwarfs</u>. New York: Harper & Row, 1967.

Lemonick, Michael D. <u>Echo Of The Big Bang</u>. Princeton (N.J.): Princeton University Press, 2003 (fairly hard). Good illustration of the interaction between research and theory in creating a scientific theory, specifically astronomy's 'big bang' theory explaining how the universe arose. Sprinkled throughout his account are glimpses of what makes scientists tick.

CHAPTER 3

Science's Rational Side

Before delving into this let us first learn a few more things about the history of modem science. First, there was the creation of science societies: the Accademia. Secretorum Naturae (Italy, 1560), Accademia dei Lincei (Italy, 1603), Accademia del Cimento (Italy, 1657), Royal Society (England, 1663), Academie des Sciences (France, 1666), Akademie der Wissenschaften (Germany, 1700), Philosophical Society of Edinburgh (Scotland, 1732), Lunar Society (England, 1766), and the Manchester Society (England, 1780). These societies enabled scientists to meet fairly regularly to swap ideas, motivate one another, develop standards for reporting on their research, arrange for their research reports to be published, and review and comment on research findings (the beginning of the peer-review process in modern science). Prior to around 1800, however, communication and collaboration among scientists were not as strong as they are today, some scientists working in isolation and thus not quite feeling themselves to be members of a 'scientific community'.

Second, the number of branches of (modern) science, or the number of sciences comprising science, mushroomed. In 1700, there were the same four as in antiquity: astronomy, physics, chemistry, and biology. Actually, physics did not exist. Rather, there were mechanics and optics. Mechanics (the study of motion and thus of moving bodies, or things) was divided into terrestrial mechanics and celestial mechanics, which dealt respectively with moving bodies on earth and above the earth (i.e., the moon and beyond). Physics as a collective name for mechanics and optics as well as for the future physics areas of hydraulics, magnetism, electricity, heat (thermodynamics), energy, etc. did not start to be used until the mid 1700s. Nor as of 1700 did biology, per se, exist. Instead, there were zoology (the study of animals) and botany (the study of plants), botany still being noticeably oriented toward medicinal needs (since doctors still used herbs for remedies). Biology as the sum total of zoology and botany as well as of the future biology areas of anatomy, biochemistry, physiology, biophysics, genetics, ethology, etc. did not come into existence until the mid 1800s. After 1700, there sprang up as new science branches/new sciences: geology, economics, and political science (circa 1775); paleontology and meteorology (circa 1800); sociology, anthropology, and archaeology (circa 1850); and psychology (circa 1875).

Third, science from 1600 onward attracted the interest, respect, and support of a growing number of well-educated and well-off Europeans, those no longer content to know only what ancient Greek scholars knew. It even became the cornerstone of a sociopolitical (social and political) movement in France spearheaded by intellectuals dubbed philosophes: Montesquieu, Voltaire, Diderot, Condorcet, etc. They wanted society guided more by science than religion and touted their movement (1690-1790) as ushering in the Age of Reason/Age of Enlightenment on how people should be treated and governed. Out of their thinking came social philosophy during the late 1700s, which about 1875 became social science. Philosophe-like notions resurfaced in the mid 1920s and variously called modern humanism(as opposed to renaissance humanism and literary humanism), empirical humanism, scientific humanism, humanistic naturalism, etc. Modern humanism is termed secular humanism by conservative Christians. Despite philosophes and modern humanists admiring science, scientists as whole did not/do not support either.

As the Age of Reason faded into the sunset there was invented the tool lathe and thus the basis for mass producing machinery. Shortly there dawned the Machine Age. It and assorted innovations stemming from new scientific knowledge gave rise to the Industrial Revolution, which began in England around 1785 and soon spread elsewhere. Upon taking root in a country this revolution drastically transformed the lifestyles and livelihoods of its citizens, putting many cottage industries out of business and forcing their owners and employees to become common laborers in factories. Factory working conditions and pay were bad. Demands for punctuality, on working uniformly, and on meeting production quotas were unknown ideas to most newcomers to factory life and caused much stress. The greatest negative impact of the Industrial Revolution was on the poor. Nevertheless, its ripples touched everyone. Aristocrats had to share power with, and were gradually undermined by, industrialists whose wealth rivaled theirs. The misery and depersonalization wrought by the revolution caused some to blame science because they saw it as having made possible many of the inventions which fueled the Industrial Revolution.

A fourth and final historical aside is about scientists. Today's image of a scientist varies from person-to-person. Yet all see a scientist as being paid, probably well, and thus see science as his job. All see, too, the cost of his research as being shouldered by someone besides him: a business, the government, foundations, etc. Many increasingly see a scientist as a woman. How does this image of a scientist compare with that of a scientist during the 1700s or 1800s? Back then, a scientist was typically a man who fell into one of two categories. He could be well off financially, coming from a rich family, and therefore able to work without pay and have his own laboratory/observatory or pay for his expedition to study, say, ancient Mayan ruins. Or he might have a wealthy patron that believed in him and in science and who gave him what he needed to conduct his research. Parenthetically, scientists in those centuries were not termed scientists, since the word scientist was not coined until 1834 and did not come into general usage until 1930. As of 1900 scientists were known as natural philosophers, scholars, astronomers, physicists, chemists, biologists, etc.

Let us start discussing science's rational side by looking again at the definition of science. On page 3 it was said:

Science is the generation of knowledge (information) by means of the integrated utilization of research and theory.

Since giving this definition we've learned a couple of things that make it more meaningful. One is that research is systematic observation taking the form of naturalistic observation (naturalistic research) or controlled observation (experimental research), a distinction predicated on whether relevant conditions are fairly uncontrolled or fairly controlled at the time observations are made. The other is that a theory, as indicated on page 22, is a relationship observed a dozen or so times and thought to be fairly well confirmed and probably true. How do research and theory dovetail?

Science does not perform its research capriciously. Rather, scientific research is guided by objectives. In basic (pure) science, the objectives are supplied by one theory or another, each objective motivating research studies designed to confirm an implication/prediction deduced from a theory. In applied science, they are furnished by one or another business project or government program that, to be successful, needs to gather information about nature, this information occasionally being eventually added to the stockpile of knowledge amassed by basic science. Thus, scientific research is shaped by theories in the case of basic science and by business projects/government programs in the case of applied science. Hence my definition of science, above, is the definition of basic science.

Theories satisfy the need to specify topics to be researched or, in other words, to determine what problems should versus shouldn't be investigated in research or, put another way, to indicate which research studies should versus shouldn't he considered worth doing. They satisfy the need to assure that scientific research never becomes an aimless, unproductive pursuit. It would be more accurate to say theories are more likely than hypotheses and laws to satisfy this need. For hypotheses, although more numerous than theories, are too unconfirmed to evince much interest from researchers, and laws, while better confirmed than theories, are typically uninteresting due to all their important implications having been deduced and researched. Consequently, scientists usually, but by no means always, pick for objectives in their studies (choose for their research problems) theoretical implications. This is why theory, not hypothesis or law, is in the definition of science.

A little more should be said about the distinctions between hypotheses, theories, and laws made on page 22. Most hypotheses do not become confirmed enough to be called theories and most theories don't become confirmed enough to be termed laws. Suppose a relationship succeeds in going from hypothesis to law. How long would this take? Newton's relationship on universal gravitation took around a hundred years, from 1685 to 1785. Ohm's relationship on the voltage, current, and resistance of electricity flowing through a circuit probably made the jump in less than five years. Darwin's relationship on speciation is still the theory of natural selection, 150 years after beginning as a hypothesis. It may never be confirmed enough to become a law. A factor determining how long it will take a relationship to go from hypothesis to theory to law, given sufficient evidence justifying its promotion, is how observable its characteristics are.

This brings me to characteristics being observed either directly or indirectly. Of course, as said earlier, we do not 'observe' characteristics. Rather, we observe things. And from observing them we imagine that the ways they are similar or dissimilar are their characteristics (e.g., color, size, and shape) and that any characteristic (e.g., color) exists in two or more states (e.g., red, yellow, and blue). Which is why psychologists refer to characteristics as mental constructs, signifying they're constructed in our minds. Nevertheless, as also pointed out earlier, we say we observe characteristics because it is difficult to say otherwise. Direct observation means observation in the everyday sense of me seeing you, you hearing a dog bark, or we both smelling smoke. Indirect observation will take more time to clarify.

We start its clarification by assuming that all observation ranges from 100% direct observation to 100% indirect observation and by assuming direct observation is direct observation whose gaps are filled by concepts—personal or impersonal—that we have imagined. Mental characteristics (e.g., intelligence, depression, memory, and concept formation) are 100% indirectly observable. So are many physical characteristics [e.g., force (like gravitation), energy (like motion), entropy, and charm (a weird name given by physicists to one type of subatomic particle)]. Occasionally the reason a characteristic is 100% indirectly observable is the thing possessing it is also 100% indirectly observable. Examples are subatomic particles: protons, electrons, neutrons, etc. Note that atoms, molecules, organelles, cells, stars beyond our Milky Way galaxy, and any planets orbiting these stars (i.e., any other solar systems) are things we originally knew only through indirect observation and that thanks to advances in technology we can now observe them directly (atoms were first seen about 1980 with a scanning-tunneling microscope). However, it would be risky to conclude that technological advances will ultimately allow us to directly observe all things.

Consider this. As a thing of interest to an observer becomes progressively more and more difficult to observe, such as seeing an ocean liner steadily moving further away from a dock from which it's being watched, the observer learns as the thing becomes still harder to see that, by doing this or that (e.g., squinting), slight differences in exactly how he observes the thing make noticeable differences in how well he observes it. Remembering what he learned here, squinting may be of value to him in the future. For if he plans to observe the same thing or a similar thing again when very difficult to observe or if he wants to tell others how they can also observe it or things like it when very hard to observe (maybe so they can confirm what he observed), then he will want to remember in detail the particular way of observing it (by squinting) that led to his best, or optimal, observations of it. Inasmuch as memory is faulty, he should carefully write down precisely what he did while observing the liner or, put more technically, precisely what operations he performed while observing it. By doing so the observer, or anybody else, can observe the thing, or things like it, in exactly the same way.

The details, or operations, just referred to are the principal ingredient in a mode of clarification known as the operational definition. An operational definition makes clear what is meant by a thing or a characteristic that is observed very indirectly. It does this by specifying in detail the way the thing or characteristic is either observed or created. Scientists wanting to remove the vagueness which allows nonmaterial forces, discussed in item 2 on page 9, to infiltrate discussions about a thing/characteristic that is far from being directly observable will claim that it is no more than its operational definition (i.e., no more than how it is observed or created). Operational definitions can take the form of a document (e.g., a test to measure the intelligence of a person or a list of steps followed to create a particular level of motivation in a laboratory rat). Also they can take the form of equipment (e.g., a voltmeter to 'measure' the voltage of a circuit or a bevatron to create antiprotons). The operational definition was invented by the American physicist Percy Bridgman in 1927. About 1935, it commenced being promoted by some psychologists. They were called operationists and their movement was known as operationism.

A relationship whose characteristics are all roughly 100% directly observable has its existence confirmed through directly observing or, simply, observing whether there is a coinciding of its characteristics. But a relationship containing at least one characteristic that is roughly 100% indirectly observable must have its existence confirmed through the more time-consuming process of confirming via (direct) observation a relationship implied by/deduced from it. Said process entails reasoning and is doable, as long as all indirectly observable characteristics are operationally defined. An approximately 100% indirectly observable characteristic that is also conceptually abstract, as opposed to concrete, prolongs the time necessary to confirm any relationship containing it because of its operational definition normally being more intricate. Gravitation in Newton's relationship is more abstract than voltage, current, and resistance in Ohm's relationship, which is partly why Newton's took longer than Ohm's to become a law.

We now resume the discussion of relationships at the bottom of page 32. Attention will focus on confirming hypothetical relationships (hypotheses) and theoretical relationships (theories) having at least one roughly 100% indirectly observable and operationally defined characteristic. Their confirmation is accomplished by observing relationships implied (predicted) by/deduced from them. Theoretical relationships of this sort inspire many research studies and guide most research performed in the name of basic science. Strictly speaking, a relationship deduced from a theory is an hypothesis while a relationship deduced from an hypothesis is a sub-hypothesis. We call all such deduced/implied/predicted relationships simply relationships in what follows.

It may seem that confirming a theoretical or hypothetical relationship of interest is a pretty straightforward job. That all depends. Four insights follow.

First, deducing a relationship from the relationship of interest is easier said than done. A researcher needs to know an interesting relationship well enough to discern what relationships exist within it and hence are deducible from it. Which means the researcher must have a knack for spotting implication. This knack might be inborn or could be cultivated, with practice. Second, a relationship deduced must be stated in a way that allows it to be either confirmed (shown probably true) or disconfirmed (shown probably false), there being no middle ground! Now confirming/disconfirming a relationship implied by a relationship of interest winds up also confirming/disconfirming this relationship of interest. The probable truth/probable falsity of a relationship deduced from an interesting relationship must be unambiguously known from observations made in a well-designed, well-conducted research study. This is what is meant by the stipulation that all deduced/implied/predicted relationships must be stated in a way which allows them to be tested/evaluated/assessed. Only relationships capable of being tested are worthwhile to science!

Third, the conclusion arrived at in the report written about a study may conclude the study's observations confirmed/disconfirmed the relationship studied (an hypothesis or a sub-hypothesis) and thereby confirmed/disconfirmed the relationship of interest (a theory or an hypothesis). Any such conclusion is open to debate. The researcher who performed the study may find that some among his peers reviewing his report do not agree with its conclusion, perhaps because they think the study wasn't well designed. Fourth, if the comments by peers disagreeing with the report's conclusion are constructive insofar as showing flaws in the study, then a researcher - the one who did the study or somebody else - may decide to redesign and redo the study.

This is a good time for us to talk about the word proven. Proven and its cognates (prove, proof, and proving) are employed in advertising, politics, and jurisprudence to characterize the truth of a statement. It has two meanings, strong and very strong. In its strong sense, proven means such-and-such is very probably true or true beyond a reasonable doubt because it is supported by reliable evidence, meaning trustworthy observations. In its very strong sense, proven means such-and-such is certainly true or true beyond the shadow of a doubt (beyond any doubt) because it is the conclusion implied by certainly true premises making up a valid deductive-type argument. Note true in its very strong sense can be justifiably applied to only conclusions validly deduced from premises addressing things that are meanings whose truths are either indisputable or assumed (e.g., the axioms/postulates underlying Euclidean geometry).

Logicians and mathematicians normally employ proven in its very strong sense. This is justified by the things they study. Popular summaries of research on television and in newspaper and magazine articles frequently claim or intimate research has proved such and-such is true. A research summary can easily mislead you into thinking that the word proven used in it means certainly true, not very probably true. Of course, ambiguity and deception are rampant in advertising. My advice is to treat 'proven' in connection with research, be it scientific or nonscientific, as meaning probably true or at most very probably true.

Theories and hypotheses are created. Occasionally, scientists say theories are constructed and hypotheses are framed. What is the difference between constructing and framing a relationship? Theory construction signifies refining a theoretical relationship (theory) in light of studies confirming/disconfirming the hypotheses implied by it and studies specifying its boundary conditions (page 23). Hypothesis framing means stating an hypothetical relationship (hypothesis). Sometimes an hypothesis is deduced from a theory; other times it is imagined, which connotes it doesn't stem from deductive reasoning. Theory construction takes more time and effort than hypothesis framing.

Every relationship has boundary conditions. They set boundaries, or limits, on the applicability of a relationship and on the situations in which we can legitimately expect to observe and thereby confirm the relationship. Boundary conditions are poorly known at the outset of a relationship's life, as an hypothesis. Yet as studies inspired by the relationship accumulate, its boundaries/limitations come to be known and more precisely specified. Boundary conditions are very much like the rules of a game. Just like it is unfair to win a game by playing it any way you want ('to play dirty pool') so, too, it is unfair to conclude a relationship was disconfirmed by a study when it is known or felt that the study's relevant conditions did not take into account the relationship's boundary conditions, as understood at the time. The expressions 'initial and boundary conditions of a theory' and 'conditions initial and boundary to a theory' refer to the causes (initial conditions) and the limits (boundary conditions) of a theoretical relationship (theory). They remind us that the theory's effect is governed by the theory's causes, within the boundaries established for the theory. A boundary problem is an issue about a theory's boundaries/limits/applicability.

Some terminology on causal relationships is noteworthy. Most of these terms were introduced during the mid 1800s by English philosopher John Stuart Mill in his treatise on the logic of science. One term is 'contributing cause'. It is germane to relationships with two or more causes. Each cause in such a relationship is viewed as contributing to the occurrence of the relationship's effect. Another term is 'necessary condition'. It is a cause that must exist in order for a relationship's effect to exist. If a relationship has one or more causes, then it has one or more necessary conditions. Still another term is sufficient condition'. A sufficient condition is the one or more causes which must exist (the one or more necessary conditions that must exist) for a relationship's effect to exist. Now an effect can have two or more sufficient conditions (two or more sets of causes, each set being one or more causes). This amounts to the same effect being in two or more relationships, each relationship having a different sufficient condition (set of one or more causes). Which is what is signified by the term 'a plurality of causes' and the expression "there is more than one means (way) to attain an end (accomplish something)." The term 'necessary and sufficient condition' means an effect has just one sufficient condition. An effect rarely, if ever, has 'a' necessary and sufficient condition. So it seems a plurality of causes is how nature (the universe) operates.

Finally, there is the term 'causal chain'. A causal chain is a sequence, series, or string of interconnected causal relationships where each relationship acts like a link in a chain. Consider a causal chain made up of three causal relationships identified as A, B, and C which take place in the order listed. The effect in A is the cause in B and the effect in B is the cause in C. Causal chains abound in nature. In fact, they are thought to be the rule, not an exception, in how causal relationships occur. Most causal chains have more than three links. Note that causal chains occurring at nearby locations in space and time can influence each other. In other words, there can be interactions between spatiotemporally proximal (nearby) causal chains.

Below is a situation where the initial cause (pesticide) led to not only the intended initial effect (killing mosquitoes) but two unforeseen, unintended subsequent effects (not killing all roaches and killing a parasite) that became the respective causes in two causal chains, each of which - through a series of causes followed by effects - ultimately ended in two unexpected side effects (threat of plague and roofs caving in):

"The World Health Organization sent pesticide to Borneo to kill mosquitoes. It worked fine, but didn't kill all of the roaches, which accumulated the pesticide in their bodies. Lizards living in the thatched huts ate the roaches. The pesticide slowed the lizards so that they were easily caught by the cats, which then died. With the cats gone, rats moved in carrying a threat of plague. In addition, the pesticide killed a type of parasite that feeds on caterpillars; the caterpillars multiplied in the huts, where they fed on the roof thatching. Then the roofs started caving in." (Reader's Digest, January 1970, p11)

This is a snapshot of a much larger chain reaction that began long before pesticide was sent to Borneo and which continued long after the mosquitoes were killed, the threat of plague arose, the roofs started caving in.

After hypotheses evolve into theories, yet before theories evolve into laws, a science (e.g., meteorology) may occasionally find that it has more than one theory/explanation of something (e.g., hurricane formation). In this situation it will keep the theory which it believes is the most fruitful and discard the other(s). Such economizing reduces the time and money spent on research designed to confirm theories. It also helps science reach its goal of explaining the things of nature by allowing a science to reduce the number of its theoretical explanations of things. Theoretical explanations are of two kinds. One is the sufficient condition of an effect, the effect's sufficient condition being its explanation. The other kind is one of three theories which is deducible from/implied by the other two, the deduced theory being the explanation of those two theories (page 22). Occasionally a theory is reconfigured to include some of the characteristics or boundary conditions in another theory, thereby allowing that theory to be eliminated. This is seen by theoretical scientists as theory construction at its best. Finding a theory which explains many things is desirable. But finding a theory explaining all things would, I think, be so general as to be of little use.

An important guideline to follow when constructing theories (theoretical explanations) is the principle of parsimony. The parsimony principle asserts we should always explain an effect in terms of a conceptually simple sufficient condition before resorting to a conceptually complex sufficient condition. A parsimonious explanation is the conceptually simplest satisfactory explanation. The principle of parsimony is a modern rendition of Occam's razor, devised in the early 1300s by English scholar William of Occam (or Ockham). A specific application of the parsimony principle was the edict that English psychologist C. Lloyd Morgan issued in 1894, known as Lloyd Morgan's canon. It declares that animal behavior ought never be explained as caused by a conceptually complex mental process if it can be satisfactorily explained as caused by a conceptually simple mental process. His canon was aimed at curbing a tendency during the late 1800s to bestow on animals the kinds of mental processes that people have. This tendency, called anthropomorphism, condones anthropomorphic explanations of animal behavior. By the way, the acronym KISS ('keep it simple, stupid'), is a fairly recent plea for us to not be unnecessarily complicated in what we think and do.

Every branch of science began with a few hypotheses which slowly grew in number. In time, most dropped by the wayside due to insufficient confirmation by research or to lack of interest in them. Of the surviving hypotheses, a few came to be theories. And of these theories, a few — very few — have thus far become laws. Recall my saying earlier that relationships deduced from a theory to confirm the theory are hypotheses and that relationships deduced from an hypothesis to confirm the hypothesis are sub-hypotheses. Now research geared to testing an hypothesis implied by a theory may, besides confirming it, be the start of a process leading to the hypothesis itself being confirmed enough to become a theory. As theories accumulate in a science there is an urge among some of its theorists to get rid of theories felt no longer worthwhile (because they are difficult to confirm any further, are largely repetitious, are narrow in scope, are incompatible with better confirmed theories or well confirmed hypotheses, etc.) and to then, where possible, combine theories. Five theories can keep fifty research scientists and a few hundred of their assistants busy for years.

All of this indicates that science is dynamic, not static, and self-correcting and that scientific knowledge ought to be viewed as tentative ideas and not eternal truths. Unlike ancient, medieval, and renaissance scientific theories, modern scientific theories are intended to be looked upon as works in progress and not as finished products. This is why we should be leery of claims science has proven such-and-such to be true (in the sense of certainly true). Nobody versed in the scientific method will say science proves anything in the sense of showing anything to be true beyond the shadow of a doubt. Indeed, most scientists steer clear of using the words prove, proven, and proof to avoid giving any such impression.

Having said so much about explanatory knowledge, we should devote a little more time to its precursors and therefore to what must exist before it can exist. Recollect that there must be descriptive knowledge before there can be explanatory knowledge and that there must be existential knowledge before there can be descriptive knowledge. Let us first look at existential knowledge.

The point I wish to make about existential knowledge is that by us now knowing the existence of countless things we should not conclude that our days of discovering things are behind us. More than once over the last 150 years it has been thought by science's admirers, even by a few scientists, that we are at the brink of knowing all there is to know about nature, only to soon have nature ruin our optimism/cockiness. Recent additions to our existential knowledge about nature suggesting plenty of new things await discovery include a multitude of life-forms with intriguing characteristics dwelling thousands of feet beneath the ocean surface, clustered around thermal (hot gas) vents on the ocean floor. Many new forms of life being found are no more than slightly different versions of small forms we presently know about, forms ranging in size from bacteria to insects. A steady stream of these 'micro' differences has furnished Darwin's theory of natural selection with its greatest confirmation. However, microevolution is not the macroevolution (one species giving rise to another species) his theory concentrates on. At the opposite end of the size spectrum of newly discovered things are stars and galaxies observed utilizing space probes and space station observatories. The first stars which appear to be hubs of solar systems were discovered around 1995.

The discovery of a thing or of a relationship between characteristics and the initial description of this thing or relationship usually take place at the same time. Follow-up studies then complete its description. While all sciences are still engaged in generating descriptive knowledge, the social sciences are much more involved in doing so than the natural sciences and hence are labeled descriptive sciences.

Describing things is characterizing them, frequently followed by classifying them. Characterizing things (e.g., hurricanes) is specifying their characteristics (e.g., wind speed) and the states of their characteristics (e.g., 60 miles per hour, 75 mph, 90 mph, 105 mph). Classifying things (e.g., rodents) is assigning them to classifications based upon their defining characteristics (e.g., teeth uniquely suited to gnawing on things). Two classifications devised by science are noteworthy: one is a taxonomy — the term for classification in biology — assembled between 1735 and 1760 by Swedish biologist Carolus Linnaeus. It splits all organisms, or life-forms, into two kingdoms (plants and animals), each kingdom into phyla, each phylum into classes, each class into orders, each order into families, each family into genera, and each genus (e.g., Homo, or man) into species (e.g., sapiens, or wise). Around 5 to 30 million species are estimated to currently exist! The other notable classification is the periodic table of chemical elements (e.g., iron, copper, sulfur, oxygen, hydrogen) pieced together about 1870 by the Russian chemist Dmitri Mendeleev. Of course, any classification is in reality a product of our imagination, since classifications are not observable.

Now describing relationships between characteristics is specifying how changes in the states of one characteristic coincide with (and, in the case of causal relationships, are due to) changes in the states of one or more other characteristics. The description of a relationship may be verbal (use words), graphic (employ a graph), or analytic (utilize an equation). Equations are preferable to words because they specify differences more precisely. However, they can't always be used. In fact, an equation is possible only if for each characteristic in a relationship it can be said that one state is greater than or less than another state by such-and-such amount. Note that the relationship referred to here, the one being described, is a theory or an hypothesis and not some relationship deduced from this theory/hypothesis.

Occasionally describing a relationship involves modeling the relationship, creating a model, simulation, or analogy of it. Normally the relationship modeled is a theory which has reached an impasse in being fully described. It is important to not confuse a model with a theory. Since a model is a partial description of a theory and not the theory in its entirety, it cannot do what a theory can do; namely, it can't explain! If a model succeeds in clarifying troublesome characteristics, then it is made a part of the theory's overall description. Alphonse Chapanis (1963) classified models as replica models (e.g., a model airplane, a ping-pong ball model of a molecule, a replica of a dinosaur, a planetarium, or a computer that imitates human learning) and symbolic models (e.g., a scale drawing of an airplane, the structural formula of a molecule, a chart of the solar system, or a mathematical model of human learning). A mathematical model is one or more equations. Modeling, or model building, has become an important activity in science.

The last aspect of science's rational side to be covered is how reason enters into designing scientific studies. Before getting into this, though, I feel it is the right time to say something I've hesitated talking about. Since around 1965 there has developed the practice in the social sciences and certain other research areas of giving naturalistic studies and experimental studies (experiments) new names. This practice refers to a naturalistic study as an observational study and to an experimental study as a controlled experiment. I prefer using the terms naturalistic study and experimental study. Why? Because to me they better indicate the difference between these two modes of research than the new names do. Specifically, the new names imply an experiment does not rely on observation and that there is such a thing as an uncontrolled experiment (historically, the defining characteristic of experimental studies is the greater control they are able to exert, compared to the control exerted in naturalistic studies).

We begin our discussion of the role played by reason in designing scientific studies by recollecting a few terms introduced earlier. One is relevant conditions (pages 26 and 27). They are all conditions in a research study that are known or suspected to influence what will be observed. Another term is control (also pages 26 and 27). Control refers to the influence a researcher exerts on conditions relevant to her study. It is seldom 0% and never 100%. Naturalistic research exerts relatively little control over relevant conditions. Experimental research exerts relatively much control over them. There are two kinds of control, physical and statistical, and two sorts of physical control, selection and manipulation. Naturalistic research utilizes control by selection (of the things to observe and the conditions under which they are observed) and, occasionally, statistical control. Experimental research uses control by selection, control by manipulation, and sometimes statistical control. Other terms are constant, variable, systematic variable, and random variable (page 27). A constant is a characteristic that exists in only one of its possible states at the time observations are made and a variable is a characteristic existing in each of two or more of its possible states when observations are performed. Characteristics can be made into constants or variables through selection or manipulation. A systematic variable is a characteristic whose states occur in a systematic, or nonrandom, fashion; a random variable is a characteristic whose states take place in a random, or unsystematic, manner. Finally, relevant conditions may now be more specifically viewed as relevant characteristics treated as relevant variables or constants and as relevant systematic or random variables. Think about this before proceeding.

Designing a scientific study entails six steps. They are outlined below. Where needed, additional terminology will be introduced and clarified.

Step 1 is settling on, followed by stating the purpose of a study or, more formally, by stating the problem/question motivating the study. If a study is intended to confirm rather than describe a theory/hypothesis, then it will also state a research hypothesis. A research hypothesis is an hypothesis/sub-hypothesis deduced from a theory/hypothesis. Intuitively, a problem/question must have a solution/answer that is testable (capable of being unambiguously evaluated) via systematic observation in order for the study to be worth doing. That a problem is not solvable via systematic observation is not always obvious. Consider the relationship (between characteristics) inspiring a study. Assume this relationship is made up of at least one characteristic which is approximately 100% indirectly observable (page 34). If the researcher designing the study does not have an adequate operational definition (page 34) of each such characteristic, then the study will be doomed.

Step 2 is deciding whether a study will be naturalistic or experimental. The decision is guided by how much control can and should be exerted (page 27) over conditions relevant to the problem stated in step 1, by the availability of resources for controlling relevant conditions, and by the researcher's expertise.

Naturalistic research embraces assorted non-experimental kinds of research that are not always distinguished from each other by widely agreed-upon names (e.g., there are, to my knowledge, no special names for the kinds of naturalistic research astronomers and meteorologists conduct). One type of naturalistic research is field research. It is done where the things of interest naturally occur and thus is performed in situ (on location). Field research gets its name from being first done by field geologists and field biologists (naturalists), whose workplace is in fields, on mountains, along rivers, and under oceans. Another type is survey research. Survey studies — surveys — are classified according to how data and information (page 26) are collected: handout surveys, mail surveys, telephone surveys, personal interview surveys. Data/information collection forms used in survey research are termed questionnaires in handout surveys and mail surveys and interview schedules in telephone and personal interview surveys. Still another type of naturalistic research is correlative research. It is geared to determining the strength of relationships, typically by utilizing statistical techniques, and is often an aspect of field and survey research. Other types of naturalistic research exist but are almost never utilized by scientists: historical research, case research, ethnographical research, and phenomenological research.

Step 3 is where a study takes shape in the researcher's mind. Decisions made in this step result in the structure of a study, its interrelated set of variables and constants. Here we must add four more kinds of variables to the systematic variables and random variables already mentioned: independent variables, dependent variables, study variables, and extraneous (nuisance/lurking) variables. An independent variable is a cause in the relationship the researcher suspects is causal. A dependent variable is the effect in this cause-effect relationship. Now if the relationship is suspected to have two contributing causes, then the study will have two independent variables. Together, the independent variable(s) and dependent variable can be regarded as study variables, since observing their relationship is the purpose of the study. Extraneous variables are variables outside a relationship between a study's independent variable(s) and dependent variable. If they influence the relationship, then the researcher will likely draw wrong conclusions about the relationship. Studies are only as good as their control of extraneous variables! Note that the relevant conditions of a study are its independent variable(s), its dependent variable, and its extraneous (nuisance/lurking) variables.

Step 4 is the decision on what will constitute data/information and the decision on how to analyze the data/information collected. Will data analysis/information analysis employ mathematical techniques and, if so, which ones? Mathematical analyses of data are commonplace these days and are frequently quite sophisticated (using, for example, nonlinear differential equations and multiple regression equations). Nonetheless, there still are studies conducted, particularly in anthropology, paleontology, and archaeology, in which mathematics plays a minor role or essentially no role at all in analyzing the data/information gathered.

Step 5 is deciding what and how many things to observe. In some research (e.g., physics and chemistry) this is a fairly easy step. But in most research it is not. The reason is that it requires picking a sampling procedure which will assure that the one or more samples obtained represent the population(s) sampled, which is a bit tricky. Several comments are in order. First, sampling procedures are also called sampling plans and sampling methods. Second, they are utilized more by some sciences (e.g., psychology and sociology) than by others. Third, names given these procedures are also given the samples generated by them: simple random sampling, stratified random samping, cluster sampling, etc. procedures yield simple random samples, stratified random samples, cluster samples, etc. Fourth, the sampling procedure chosen is partly determined by the requirements of any statistical techniques decided on in step 4. Steps two through five in designing a scientific study address what's called research methodology: techniques/procedures to control relevant conditions, to draw samples, to collect data, and to analyze data.

Step 6, the last step, is an assortment of decisions about equipment and data/information collection forms; on whether to buy, build, or (if lucky) borrow things needed; about how acceptable the validity and reliability are of the measuring devices (including psychological tests) to be used; on the desirability of conducting a little 'pilot study' before performing the main study — the one being designed — in order to gather information that will enhance the quality of the main study; etc. Decisions made about such matters put finishing touches on the blueprint of a study.

References

Becker, Carl L. The Heavenly City Of The Eighteenth-Century Philosophers. New Haven: Yale University Press, 1932 (fairly easy). An excellent look at thinking which characterized the Age of Reason, or Age of Enlightenment, and how this thinking gave valuable support to natural philosophy and, during the late 1700s, inspired the birth of social philosophy (which in the late 1800s became social science).

Beveridge, William I. B. The Art of Scientific Investigation. New York: Vintage Books, 1957 (second edition) (fairly easy). Case studies from biology showing how observation, reason, and intuition have meshed to generate significant research findings by identifying fruitful research questions/problems to answer/solve. Well worth reading.

Chapanis, Alphonse Men, Machines, and Models. In Marx, M. H. (Editor) Theories in Contemporary Psychology. New York: Macmillan, 1963, pp 104-129.

Copi, Irving M. and Cohen, Carl Introduction To Logic. New York: Macmillan, 1994 (ninth edition) (fairly hard). A good account of language, deductive logic, inductive logic, and the use of logic in science and jurisprudence.

Taton, René Reason And Chance In Scientific Discovery. New York: Science Editions, 1962 (fairly easy). Similar in purpose to, hut covering more fields of science than Beveridge's book. It, too, is well worth reading.

CHAPTER 4

Scientific And Nonscientific Views On Nature

The first three chapters conveyed the essence of modern science as an activity during the 1600s and 1700s and as a social institution from roughly 1850 onward, a social institution dedicated to explaining the things in nature the universe and the changes they undergo. We saw in those chapters that the explanatory knowledge science wants most is built upon descriptive knowledge and that descriptive knowledge is founded on existential knowledge. Also, we learned that these three aspects of scientific knowledge. are generated using the scientific method and that it is this method which defines science and contrasts it with other activities and social institutions. Moreover, we saw that a consensus on what the scientific method is and a scaling back of what was traditionally meant by 'the sciences' occurred around 1875, when the scientific method began to be increasingly viewed as the integrated utilization of research and theory.

Despite scientists having staked the claim to be the authorities on knowing nature, they are neither alone nor the first in making this claim. Now that we understand science and the scientific method we can look into the knowledge and beliefs about nature which have arisen out of activities and social institutions that use methods other than science's method. Therefore, our attention will next be directed at views that compete with those of science or are wrongly labeled, sometimes deliberately, scientific. In what follows we will use the words view and viewpoint interchangeably to signify knowledge and beliefs about nature and will restrict ourselves to summarizing clearly contentious conflicts concerning scientific and nonscientific views on nature.

Maybe a good place to start is with personal knowledge. For it includes a person's current thoughts and feelings about scientific knowledge. These thoughts and feelings are based upon what a person knows about science in general, a science, or a topic in a science. His/her thoughts and feelings arise from all sorts of experiences and range, in gradations, from disliking to liking science, a science, or a topic in a science. Therefore, each reader is apt to already have a personal opinion about some of the assorted views to be discussed.

Shamans, medicine men, medicine women, and witchdoctors since prehistoric times and wise men, wise women, priests, and priestesses since historic times made knowing nature part of their job of serving members of their communities. To know nature was to know how to mend a sick or injured body, to heal a troubled or possessed soul, and foretell/forecast/predict events benevolent and malevolent to a person or a community. Knowing nature meant knowing how to talk nature spirits and, later, gods into making nature give people or communities what they asked for, such know-how taking the form of rituals, incantations, sacrifices, and prayers. Foretelling was done in many ways. One was watching the night sky, especially at specific locations along the horizon just before sunrise or after sunset, to spot slight changes in the positions of certain stars, planets, or constellations (configurations of stars). Eventually, the cumulative knowledge passed from generation to generation resulted in specialization. Two early specialties were medicine (circa 9000 B.C.) and astronomy (circa 3000 B.C.), astronomy in Babylonia giving rise to astrology around 1600 B.C. These specialties were the respective professions of the physician (doctor) and the priest-astronomer.

We may feel the knowledge and beliefs about nature held by these early predecessors of today's physicians and astronomers, as well as how their views were arrived at, to be crude (even laughable) and minimize them like we are inclined to do regarding the play of children. Yet it should be realized that a child's play is not merely a child having fun. It is often serious business to a child, as it rightfully should be inasmuch as it is the start of learning about nature in the sense of learning about those things in nature named Mom, Dad, food, bed, danger, etc. Also playing is one means of developing the patience and skill at observing and reasoning needed to generate knowledge about nature. Much can be learned watching children at play or, should I say, children at work. All too often we adults ignore the value of what a child does as well as what an adult 100, 1000, or 10,000 years ago did.

When knowledge about nature reaches a certain point in a culture, there emerges a view of the world. This worldview, or big picture, is a mixture of knowledge and belief which is intended to explain how a person, tribe, village, city, or nation fits into nature/the universe. Its function is to satisfy curiosity and allay fear. By around the year 1300 there existed in much of Europe a worldview describable thusly:

"----- the world and all that's in it was created for the service of man, and mam had been created for the service of God.----- The sun was there to give us light and to tell the time and mark out the calendar by its motions. The stars and planets were a means of distributing beneficent and maleficient influences to the things on earth to which they were sympathetically linked: plants and animals were there to give us food and pleasure, and we were there to please God by doing his will." (Taylor, 1963, p 131)

This teleological explanation of existence gave purpose and comfort to life. It was a view inspired by Aristotelianism/Aristotelian philosophy.

Recall (page 6) that Aristotle's far-ranging, largely rational philosophy was accepted by the Roman Catholic Church in the late 1200s. From about 1300 onward the Catholic Church promoted Aristotelian philosophy, in the form of Thomism. The Church did this because it felt Aristotelianism would end one of several sources of growing unhappiness with the Church. These sources were as follow. Clergy and laity were sick of Church corruption. Noblemen and kings were mad at the Church inserting itself more and more into secular affairs they regarded their bailiwicks. Spiritually unquenched peasants and eccentrics were leaving the Church in droves, some adopting more fulfilling alternate beliefs such as Catharism (gnostic-type sects), witchcraft (Satanism/Devil worship), magic, neo-Platonism, alchemy, astrology, proto-Protestant sects (e.g., Waldenses and, around 1400, Hussites), and Cabalism. Lastly, a rising tide of European intellectuals resented the Church discouraging them from reading the influx of Arabic-to-Latin translations of hitherto unknown or poorly known manuscripts on ancient Greek and medieval Moslem knowledge about nature and other subjects. These manuscripts posed a serious threat to the Church's image of omniscience. By accepting Aristotelianism, which embraced so much knowledge, the Church hoped to placate intellectuals and thereby maintain, if not strengthen, its authority in Europe. Incidentally, the expression medieval Moslem knowledge means knowledge generated during the intellectual heyday of the Moslem, or Islamic, Empire and thus from 800 to 1200 approximately.

The first major competition between scientific and nonscientific views on nature took place in astronomy. It was between supporters of astronomy's long accepted geocentric theory and advocates of heliocentric theory (page 25). Geocentric theory was part of Aristotle's philosophy. His particular version of it was based upon a geocentric theory. conceived twenty years earlier by the Greek astronomer Eudoxos. About 500 years later the Greek astronomer Ptolemy improved Aristotle's theory, enabling it to more precisely describe movements of those celestial bodies called planets. The result was Ptolemy's geocentric theory. Aristotle's and Ptolemy's theories are considered today to respectively be a speculation and a model, not theories. Their 'theories' were increasingly challenged after 1530 by the supporters of a heliocentric theory set forth by the Polish astronomer Nicholas Copernicus.

Copernicus' heliocentric theory caused little stir during the mid and late 1500s. Then in about 1600 the Church started to firmly defend the Aristotelian/Ptolemaic theory and denounce the Copernican theory, which was still an hypothesis. There were two reasons for this. First, the Church feared heliocentrism would strengthen the beliefs of heretics and eccentrics (potential heretics). For in the 1590s it had appealed to the renegade cleric and philosopher Giordano Bruno. Second, the Church said that Copernicus claimed the earth does things-moving around the sun and spinning on its axis-which the Bible says earth doesn't do. Passages from Scripture were cited attesting to earth being motionless. Around 1610 the physicist and astronomer Galileo commenced extolling the Copernican theory after recently making a number of telescopic observations that he interpreted as confirming it. Galileo's support of the theory from 1615 to 1633 increasingly got him into trouble with the Church's Holy Inquisition (ecclesiastical court) and finally with Pope Urban VIII. He lived the remaining nine years of his life under house arrest. Three comments are in order about the heliocentrism-geocentrism controversy, which persisted until 1650.

One is that the first competition between scientific and nonscientific views on nature was also the first altercation between science (natural philosophy) and Christian religion. Another is that the Copernican heliocentric theory was only a little more scientific than the Ptolemaic/Aristotelian geocentric theory. Its acceptance by Galileo and the German astronomer Johannes Kepler was due to it explaining celestial motion just as well as the geocentric theory did, maybe even better, and doing so in a conceptually and technically simpler fashion. They did what parsimony urges (page 39). But we should realize that Copernicus' view of the solar system isn't ours. The reason why is it was based upon Aristotle's physics (which assumed the sun, moon, and planets move in circular orbits around the earth) and Ptolemy's technique of using circular orbits and epicycles to describe the circular movements of the sun, moon, and planets. Even though Copernican heliocentrism had Ptolemy's circular orbits and epicycles, it reduced their number down to 34. My third comment is that between 1609 and 1619 Kepler modernized Copernicus' theory by replacing its circular orbits and epicycles with seven elliptical orbits, one each for our moon and the six planets known back then: Mercury, Venus, earth, Mars, Jupiter, Saturn. He therefore largely gave us what nowadays we know as our solar system. The elliptical shape of the orbits along which planets go around the sun and along which the moon goes around the earth were explained in about 1685 by Newton's hypothesis of universal gravitation.

The second major competition between scientific and nonscientific views on nature was between the vitalistic and reductionistic (mechanistic) views regarding life, whose proponents are called vitalists and reductionists/mechanists/molecular biologists). Vitalism is the nonscientific view. It's traceable to Aristotle. He believed terrestrial things, meaning earth and all things on and in it, are made of blends of four essences/elements/elementary substances. Listed in order of decreasing density, they are earth, water, air, and fire. He also thought celestial things the sun, moon, other planets, and stars - are made of a fifth essence, or quintessence (quint means five), far less dense than fire. It is ether. Finally, he felt terrestrial things that are alive differ from those which are not by possessing tiny amounts of an essence which is nearly the same in density, fineness, or subtlety as ether; namely, the essence vital heat. On page 7 we said Aristotle assumed nature to be a continuous substance having no void. This can be reworded to say that for him nature is an uninterrupted expanse of material (i.e., matter) and material energy (i.e., the energy derived from matter). Which means we can say that by vital heat Aristotle meant a material force (energy). But why bother?

The reason for bothering is despite Aristotle being a vitalist due to his thinking something distinguishes life from nonlife (the vital from the nonvital) he was not a vitalist in the modern sense of the word. Now in modern times, commencing about 1700, a few people began to construe Aristotle's material vital heat as something that is nonmaterial (i.e., as a thing which is neither matter nor energy derived from matter). Around 1820, they started being known as vitalists. The first of these modern vitalists was Georg Stahl, a German chemist. In about 1700 Stahl became convinced all living things have souls, a notion he could have gotten from Aristotle's theory of souls.

Aristotle's soul theory speculates that all living things have a soul, anima (in Latin), or psyche (in Greek). Details about a soul's function/functioning/activity vary with the basic form of the life that possesses it. He said the soul in all life-forms has a vegetative (nutritive) function — it performs vegetative activities — allowing them to grow and to reproduce. The soul in animals has a vegetative function and a sensory-motor function, the latter allowing them to sense things and to move. The soul in humans has a vegetative function, a sensory-motor function, and an intellectual function, the latter permitting them to be intelligent and to think rationally. Aristotle said that the soul in a living thing ceases to exist when the thing dies, except for the intellectual aspect of the human soul. He intimates that upon death a person's personality merges with a super soul (God?). What's germane to this discussion is Aristotle's notion that the vegetative function of a soul generates vital heat.

Stahl could have also been influenced by iatrochemistry. Iatrochemistry was a view on medicine popular between 1525 and 1675. It assumed three things. First, everything is alive. Second, the life residing in a medicine is what allows this medicine to cure ailments. Third, medicines prepared from minerals are generally more effective than those prepared from herbs (herbal medicines). The first two assumptions show the mystical leanings of iatrochemists, the most zealous of whom were the Swiss doctor and chemist Paracelsus and the Belgian doctor and chemist van Helmont.

The modern vitalists who arose around 1700 thought living things, unlike nonliving things, have a *nonmaterial* something, without which death occurs. From 1700 to 1850, they conceived it to be a nonmaterial force or energy referred to as the life force, vital force, force hypermechanique, elan vital, etc. Advances in biochemistry and physiology after 1825 undermined the need to explain life by invoking nonmaterial forces, leading to vitalism's demise about 1850. Then, around 1900, vitalism was resurrected and renamed neovitalism. Neovitalism replaced vitalism's nonmaterial life force with a nonmaterial formative, or holistic, principle and tried to justify the principle by saying a living thing is more than its material parts and their interactions, said principle being this 'nonmaterial more than'. Continued progress in biochemistry and physiology led to neovitalism biting the dust about 1950. The better known vitalists (1700-1850), after Georg Stahl, were the French doctors Theophile de Bordeu, Paul Barthez, and Xavier Bichat; Swedish chemist Jöns Berzelius; and German physiologist Johannes Müller. The key neovitalists (1900-1950) were English physiologist John Haldane and German embryologist Hans Driesch. Driesch referred to the formative/holistic principle as the entelechy (signifying that it is mind-like). Entelechy is a word Aristotle coined.

As an aside, vitalism was more popular outside than inside science. It had a special appeal to romanticists. Romanticists were a group of mystically inclined poets, artists, and philosophers (Goethe, Blake, Shelley, Kierkegaard, etc.) who were active between 1790 and 1840. Their outlook, romanticism, was a reaction to the thinking associated with the Age of Reason, Newtonian determinism, the materialistic orientation of science, and the material values in society, all of which had by 1790 come to strongly influence much of Europe.

Now the scientific view about life is reductionism or, equivalently, mechanism. Its advocates are called reductionists and mechanists. They are physiologists and molecular biologists (i.e., biochemists and biophysicists). How did reductionism come to be? Let me digress briefly to set the stage for its debut.

Doctors since ancient Egyptian times have known human and animal bodies have a structure. By this is meant their bodies consist of parts, some external (always observed) and others internal (rarely observed). They've known too that body parts have a function. Now while function can be a synonym for purpose, it can also signify activity (e.g., what a body part does). By function and functioning is meant the activity of a body part and especially the integrated activity of body parts, be this the coordinated movements of external parts (e.g., arms, legs, and fingers), the flow of blood through blood vessels, or the passage of ions (atoms with electric charges) across the membranes surrounding cells in a body. Since activity is motion and mechanics is the study of motion and since physics was increasingly regarded the epitome of science, biologists who wanted to study the function/functioning of a body's parts commenced in the 1700s naming their profession mechanics and themselves mechanists. Around 1850, their profession and they would be renamed physiology and physiologists.

Reductionism arose in response to what biologists learned after 1700. They learned that explaining the function of bodies (general physiology) requires knowing the function of tissues making up bodies (tissue physiology), that knowing tissue function depends on knowing the function of the cells constituting tissues (cell physiology), that knowing how cells function rests on knowing the function of the molecules comprising them (molecular biology), and that knowing all these things is governed by a variety of technological breakthroughs. This in a nutshell is how reductionism arose.

Biochemists and physiologists did research between 1825 and 1950 which steadily demonstrated that there is no need to explain what interested them by resorting to the nonmaterial somethings of vitalism and neovitalism. To them, their reductionistic, or physicochemical, explanations were quite adequate. From 1825 onward, the number of reductionists in biology grew. Their view on life became the view in biology about 1850. Notable reductionists from 1830 to 1890 included — all Germans — the chemist Justusvon Liebig, physiologist Karl Ludwig, physiologist Emil Du Bois-Reymond, and physicist-physiologist Hermann von Helmholtz.

The third and fourth major competitions were between two scientific views and two nonscientific views about natural history. Natural history is the story of the origin of earth, life, and the universe as well as subsequent changes in them. The third major competition was between the Bible's view and geology's view on the history of earth while the fourth was between the biblical view and biological view on the history of life. Both religious views are in the first book, Genesis, of the Old Testament of the Bible. They say the origin of earth and life on it was their creation by God. Geology's and biology's views say the origin of earth and life was their evolution. Evolution sees earth and life on it as today being the latest stage in geological and biological processes driven by innumerable causally-related activities. The theories of geological evolution were formulated between 1785 and 1840 whereas the theories of biological evolution were set forth between 1810 and 1870. What follows is a look at theories about evolution developed by geologists and biologists.

Geology's view stems from efforts to explain the occasionally observed, roughly horizontal layering's (stratifications) of land, seashells sometimes imbedded in these layers (strata), and orderly differences in the types of shells in one versus another layer (stratum). Now as the 1600s gave way to the 1700s there ended 400 years of Aristotle being widely regarded the authority on nature and of the stifling effect which this had had on any desire to know more than the master knew. One result, around 1700, was a burst of interest in knowing nature, particularly in discovering new things of a geological or biological kind, and the debut of nature buffs who studied rocks, caves, glaciers, land strata, plants, animals, etc. and who, if their observations were systematic, were called natural philosophers. Part of this interest arose from steadily learning more about the fascinating things explorers and then settlers were discovering in such faraway places as the Americas, the Pacific Islands, southeast Asia, etc. Compared to the Roman Catholic Church, the Protestant Churches which split from it during the 1500s and 1600s (e.g., the Lutherans, Anabaptists, Mennonites, Calvinists, Anglicans, Presbyterians, Congregationalists, Baptists, etc.) were generally more tolerant of people being curious about nature and occasionally even welcomed such curiosity.

Initially, natural philosophers coming across the aforementioned layers, scientists we'd today refer to as field geologists and field biologists (naturalists), assumed their origin was the global flood described in the Bible. For although Aristotelian knowledge about nature was by 1700 no longer accepted, whatever the Bible said or implied about nature, or anything was still accepted. Aristotle's authority was no more, Roman Catholic authority had waned, but biblical authority ruled supreme! So it was natural to look at these strata as artifacts of the biblical Flood/Deluge. If something did not make sense to them, then these natural philosophers, who were Christians first, blamed it on a lack of their ability to correctly understand what the Bible said or implied about nature. Never did they blame it on errors of commission or omission in the Bible. It may seem odd to many people today but back in the early and mid 1700s there was a sincere, largely Protestant desire to discover all the many things geological and biological that God had created. The purpose was to behold the full splendor of earth and thereby to more fully appreciate its creation and its Creator.

Beginning around 1785, the attitude towards the biblical account started to change. The cause was a growing difficulty ascribing the mounting disparities between what was observed and what the Bible said to an inability to understand the Bible. Repeated reading and reflecting upon its passages led increasing numbers of natural philosophers, some of them knowing the Bible quite well, to conclude that the Bible neither explicitly nor implicitly addressed most of what puzzled them about land strata, seashells in them, and the orderliness in the distribution of shell types within and between strata. Hence, it appeared that the Bible had errors (of omission). This came as a shock to many people. What followed was tension between geology and Christianity and, shortly, greater tension between biology and Christianity. Actually, it is more accurate to say these tensions were between natural philosophers who no longer saw the Bible as an accurate portrayal of nature and those ministers/priests, laborers, merchants, other natural philosophers, etc. who continued acknowledging the Bible as complete and error-free.

The layers, or strata, just mentioned are made of sediments (i.e., aggregates of sand, pebbles, gravel, and decomposed things that once lived). Seashells embedded in them are instances of what are known as fossils, fossilized remains, or undecomposed remains of once living things. During the late 1700s there began being discovered fossils a lot more perplexing than these seashells. A little imagination showed them to be remnants of plants and animals that, when alive, looked quite different from the plants and animals of modern times. Assuming a stratum of interest was laid down, or formed, later in time than the stratum underneath it and assuming from what is known about current rates of sedimentation or sediment formation (e.g., in lakes) that it probably took a very long time for the stratum of interest to form, many geologists concluded two things.

First, the lower strata must have been formed much longer ago than the age of earth arrived at utilizing chronologies pieced together from genealogies (lineages) in the Book of Genesis, the respected Irish Protestant Archbishop James Ussher having in 1650 estimated earth was created in 4004 B.C. By contrast, a scientist in about 1775 estimated that earth was created as far back as 75,000 B.C. Around 1800, another scientist said the earth is likely a hundred million years old. Today, science estimates earth to be roughly 4.5 billion years old. Second, some plants (e.g., giant fern trees) and animals (e.g., dinosaurs) arose long after earth had been created and disappeared long before man's creation, judging from strata containing versus not containing their fossils. Thus, earth had over the millennia seen species come and go. Yet the biblical account of natural history gave the impression that no major changes in earth's geology or biology had taken place since its creation, except for the flood/deluge.

Geological research implied that the aforementioned disparities could be reconciled by explaining them as being the result of geological evolution. So thought the English geologist, James Hutton. Hutton framed an hypothesis on geological evolution in 1785 and fine-tuned it in 1795. In the 1830s, his hypothesis was modified and popularized by the English geologist Charles Lyell. Geological findings and their explanation in terms of Lyell's theory of geological evolution upset some Christians. Many more would be unhappy with Darwin's theory of biological evolution.

Biological evolution started to be entertained during the late 1700s. The first idea about it to become a theory was that of the French naturalist Jean Lamarck. Announced in 1809, it was called the theory of acquired (states of) characteristics due to its viewing biological evolution as a species undergoing changes by offspring inheriting, or acquiring, the beneficial (states of) characteristics of their parents, improving upon (states of) these characteristics slightly as they matured, and passing these improvements on to their offspring, which repeated the process. The theory, more aptly labeled an hypothesis, explained, say, the supposed lengthening of a giraffe's neck from one generation to the next which allowed giraffes to reach and eat leaves higher up in trees than could giraffes a few generations earlier. Most biologists showed little interest in Lamarck's theory, also called Lamarckian evolution and Lamarckism. Thus, it largely dropped by the wayside and did not noticeably trouble devout Christians. This was not the case with Darwinism, Darwinian evolution, or, more precisely, Darwin's theory of (descent through) natural selection. His theory is what ordinarily comes to mind whenever one hears the term biological evolution.

Charles Darwin, an English naturalist, published his theory in 1859. Its gist is this. First, any *organism* (living thing) which by way of chance inheritance, or inheriting (states of) characteristics on a random basis, comes to possess more useful (states of) characteristics than useless or harmful ones will more likely be suited to and hence be able to survive longer within its particular environmental niche than will an organism whose chance inheritance gave it more useless or harmful (states of) characteristics than useful ones. Second, *any species* of organism whose members are likely to survive long enough to bear offspring is more likely to endure than is a species whose members are less likely to live that long. Basically the theory says 'nature' creates new and destroys old species by selecting which members of a species will have which (states of what) characteristics, predicating its selection figuratively speaking on the role of dice. It pictures nature as creating new species out of existing species. A very rough cultural analogue of this would be some Italians (one species) immigrating during the late 1800s and early 1900s to America and then over a period of three generations becoming by the fourth generation culturally distinct Italian-Americans (another species).

Since there had been rising excitement among natural philosophers in the early and mid 1800s over discoveries of fossils of enormous prehistoric animals and, during the mid 1800s, of prehistoric humans too, the climate was ripe for a theory explaining the evolution of species across an interval of time spanning hundreds of thousands of years. And since the main desire back then was to come up with an explanation of the more obvious differences between organisms, such as those between apes and humans, the thrust of Darwin's theory was to explain macroevolution — speciation — and thus the evolution of one species of animal or plant life into another.

Darwinian evolution got support from Lyell, who by 1859 was influential in natural philosophy, and much support from the English biologist Thomas Huxley, whose zeal in promoting the theory earned him the nickname Darwin's bulldog. The theory increased the confirmation of biological evolution. But only a few biologists accepted the theory as the explanation of evolution, until the mid 1940s. That is when research in genetics and molecular biology reached the point of making the theory more credible. Darwinism rapidly incurred the wrath of conservative Christians (at that time most Christians were conservative). In the early 1900s, evolution started to be mentioned in science courses taught in America's public schools. This stopped after 1925 due to a school teacher in Tennessee, John Scopes, being brought to trial for breaking a state law that forbid teaching evolution in Tennessee's public schools.

In the late 1950s, evolution started again being taught in public schools. This was met by objections from conservative Christians, especially Protestant fundamentalists. When their objections went unheeded, fundamentalists tried requiring biblical Creation taught wherever evolution is taught. They failed because Creation isn't a scientific view on nature. Moreover, being a religious view on nature, teaching it in public schools (all of them get federal money) amounts to teaching religion in public schools. And to teach religion in public schools is unconstitutional because the U.S. Constitution insists upon a clear separation of Church (religion) and State (government). Undaunted, fundamentalists in the early 1960s launched a movement geared to amassing evidence against evolution and, so they reasoned, for Creation. Evidence was soon forthcoming and led them to promote what they termed scientific creationism, or creation science, and to marketing textbooks asserting or intimating that scientific creationism has produced well confirmed scientific knowledge. Most scientists see little science in creation science, dismissing it as thinly veiled biblical creationism. They are right in light of the extent to which creation scientists do not generate knowledge about nature scientifically and thus by utilizing the scientific method. What's more, creation scientists feel that by disconfirming one theory (evolution) they automatically confirm an alternate theory (creation). This is not true! Now in science there is, at least in principle, the spirit of allowing observation as free a reign as possible to lead the way in determining the probable truth of this or that contending theory/hypothesis, an ideal not always witnessed in the practice of science and essentially absent from the practice of creation science.

The uproar over biological evolution in general and Darwinian biological evolution in particular continues. As conflicts between science and religion go, the Darwin affair far surpasses in bitterness and duration the Galileo affair. Yet the uproar here isn't just between rival religious and scientific views on natural history. For although Darwin's theory enjoyed increasing support from scientists throughout the mid 1900s, storm clouds within science unrelated to religiosity began to gather during the late 1900s. Today, his theory is seen in the halls of science as not quite as well confirmed as once thought, even after taking into account its revision in 1972 to include punctuated equilibria, or evolution in spurts. The theory's greatest confirmation is in explaining microevolution. Now although evidence for microevolution is an important scientific finding, microevolution is far from the macroevolution whose explanation was the theory's purpose and upon which the theory's probable truth ought to be judged.

Amidst the clamor over biological evolution there appeared in the early 1900s two views that became vexations for Christianity (and Judaism). One took root on the fringe of science and involved Sigmund Freud, an Austrian psychiatrist. Freud's treatment of women suffering from the mental disorder hysteria, a type of neurosis fairly common in European women of the late 1800s and early 1900s, prompted him around 1900 to hypothesize three things. One hypothesis was these hysterias are driven by a sexual energy he called libido that is due to memories of sexual sensations experienced as an infant. A second was these memories are unconscious and hence unknown to the person possessing them, unless a therapist facilitates their entering into consciousness in order to work on them. The third was these unconscious sexual memories are an important motivator of behavior and thus are the unconscious motivation behind much of behavior. Put another way, the third hypothesis asserts behavior is motivated by things we are largely not aware (conscious) of and for that reason, so it seems, are largely unable to do anything about. Actually these three hypotheses were sub-hypotheses within one hypothesis, an hypothesis about neurotic behavior. This hypothesis became a theory around 1910, the Freudian theory/explanation of neuroses.

After 1910 Freud's theory caught the attention of people from various walks of life. Some found it profound. Others found it profane. Many religious leaders found it to be unsettling. Their concern was this. People of faith have as their ultimate goal in life, the goal to which all other goals are subordinate, obeying the articles of their faith. Which for Christians and Jews means obeying the Bible. Love of God and accepting Jesus as their (soul's) way to God and Heaven following their death are paramount to Christians and to ministers and priests offering them spiritual guidance.

Christians, Jews, and Muslims belong to faiths which see people as having volition, or free-will, and thus having control over their thoughts and actions. Such individuals. are regarded as being accountable for thinking and doing bad things. The opposite of being free to choose what to think and how to act is not being free to do so, due to our thoughts and actions being determined/caused by things beyond our control. If determinism/causation exerts an influence on human thought and action, then, to the extent it does, we don't have free-will (freedom of choice). Without that freedom, how accountable are we for any bad things we think and do? If people do not feel they have freedom to control their thoughts and actions, then they will not see themselves as having a say in getting to Heaven and thus will not consider the 'thou shalt nots' of religion to be worth heeding! This is the determinism versus indeterminism issue in philosophy that we met on page 24.

To the degree Freud's theory caught on, to that degree people could relinquish responsibility for their thoughts and actions. And with attaining Heaven no longer seen as contingent on what they think and do, people would probably gravitate toward thinking and doing more bad things than before. It is this that religious leaders found alarming about Freudian theory. For they felt most people learning of the theory would interpret it as telling them to not worry what they think and do inasmuch as thinking and doing are governed/determined/caused by unconscious memoires of sexual sensations traceable to when they were infants and largely unable to yet know right from wrong.

The second vexation for Judeo-Christianity was a school (orientation) in psychology called behaviorism. Like Freud's theory, it is a scientific view on nature. Here, though, we are dealing with a methodological view, a specific way to best know a subject (i.e., animal and human behavior). Behaviorism was founded in 1913 by the American psychologist John Watson. Prior to founding it, he had belonged to a school in psychology known as functionalism. Functionalism studied a wide variety of behavioral and mental topics: learning, memory, perception, motivation, intelligence, etc. A few functionalists studying the learning, perception, and motivation of animals explained their observations in terms of human mental processes. This irritated Watson, like it had irritated C. Lloyd Morgan in 1894 (page 39). He left functionalism to pioneer behaviorism. Watson saw behaviorism to be the study of 100% directly observable behavior (muscle flexions and gland secretions) in animals and humans. Conversely, behaviorism isn't to be the study of 0% directly observable mental processes (learning, memory, perception, etc.) which functionalists assume are the basis of all behavior. He was particularly unhappy with one mental process, consciousness. Watson inspired numerous psychologists to become behaviorists. Behaviorism was very popular from 1920 to 1970. About 1935, it gave rise to the operationist movement in psychology (page 34).

Watson didn't deny consciousness exists, just the fruitfulness of studying it. His goal was to identify relationships between stimuli (causes) and responses (effects). This is how behaviorism got to be also called stimulus-response and S-R psychology. Several forms of behaviorism sprouted between 1930 and 1960. One became quite popular during the 1950s and 1960s. It was conceived by the American psychologist B.F. Skinner. His specific approach to studying behavior, termed the experimental analysis of behavior, was Watson's dream come true. Most of Skinner's research was performed on rats and pigeons. Yet some was done on humans. It was his human studies that would become contentious. Skinnerian behaviorism disturbed most religious people and some atheists. Why? Because it viewed humans, like it did animals, as no more than black boxes. A black box is an electric or electronic circuit enclosed inside an often black box, which hides it from view. Its functioning is assessed by observing inputs to it, outputs from it, and the resulting input-output function (relationship). Although the term white box is rarely used, it means something whose innards can be seen. Now by treating animals and humans as black boxes Skinner ignored what's inside them (mental processes and biological processes) and thus what was going on inside them. He did this because he felt knowing such things is irrelevant to knowing behavior and diverts our attempts to know behavior. His methodological stance was opposite that of cognitive psychology (which studies mental processes, mainly in humans) and physiological psychology/biopsychology (which studies neural, hormonal, and other biological processes). Applied to humans, it was dehumanizing and repugnant to many people.

From what has been said thus far in this chapter it might appear most nonscientific views on nature are those associated with religion. That is because the oldest, loudest, furthest reaching disagreements concerning scientific and nonscientific views on nature have so far in our account usually involved nonscientific views which happen to also be religious views, the lone exception being vitalism. During the remainder of the chapter we look at some more competition between scientific and nonscientific views, those not associated with religion. We'll concentrate on views which, like creation science, have masqueraded as science because their advocates say or intimate they are either scientific views or have been well confirmed by scientific research. These views are commonly referred to by scientists as pseudoscientific views and as examples of pseudoscience, "pseudo" meaning false.

Modern science went from being an activity to a social institution in about 1850. While by 1850 science was generally well respected, it becoming a social institution made it more so. The ensuing greater respect accorded science led nonscientists who wanted receptive audiences for their views (or services or merchandise or whatever) to steadily capitalize on the prestige of science by linking their views in the public eye to science. This became a problem for science and worrisome to scientists from the late

1800s onward. For if nonscientific things are perceived to be scientific things by the public and if these things are eventually shown untrue (or not up to par or downright harmful), then a public that doesn't know the difference between what is scientific and what is nonscientific is apt to blame science for leading them astray, to the detriment of science and scientists. Exposing pseudoscience for what it is started to be done during the early 1900s. A classic book on pseudoscience written by Martin Gardner came out in 1952. Its second edition (1957), which is still informative, covers such topics (i.e., views, services, or merchandise) as the submerged continents of Atlantis and Lemuria, the ideas that earth is flat or hollow, Lysenko's phasic development of plants, Reich's orgone energy and orgonomy, Velikovsky's celestial cataclysm theory, and dianetics (today called scientology).

A more recent exposé of pseudoscientific views is the article from which the following has been excerpted:

> "We've been haunted by a hot-selling book called the Amityville Horror, intrigued by the Bermuda Triangle, mystified by tales of ancient astronauts, entertained by the exploits of psychokinetic key benders, assailed by mail-order ads for biorhythm calculators, comforted by tales of out-of-body and post-death experiences, regaled by stories of conversations with plants, unnerved by accounts of Bigfoot, the abominable snow man and the Loch Ness monster, and stupefied by reports of burst appendixes removed sans scalpels.------

> "The more conventional-minded among us are starting to ask what is going on. Why the sudden explosion of interest, even among some otherwise sensible people, in all sorts of paranormal "happenings"? Are we in retreat from the scientific ideals of rationality, dispassionate examination of evidence and sober experiment that have made modem civilization what it is? Has the West lost its unique drive to find the closest approximation of objective truth?

> " -------some scientists are beginning to fight back. They have even gone so far as to set up an organization-The Committee for the Scientific Investigation of Claims of the Paranormal, CSICP for short-to investigate unusual phenomena without bias and to help the public distinguish between what evidence is

valid and what is invalid, between legitimate questions and manufactured mysteries, between fact and sheer fiction." (Frazier, 1978, p 55)

This article and Gardner's book go beyond exposing such-and-such as pseudoscientific. For after exposing it they then typically proceed to destroy its credibility, an activity termed debunking. Their debunking gives the impression the view being debunked is no good not only because it pretends to be a scientific view but because it is not a scientific view, implying only scientific views on nature are good views.

We see in Frazier's language a potential for abuse. The abuse becomes actual if debunking is done to views solely because they were set forth by people who are not regarded scientists by established, accepted, mainstream, or orthodox science and thus by the scientific establishment. Debunking is appropriate only if a view masquerades as a scientific view and is not a scientific view, either because it cannot be tested or because its author has no intention of it being tested. Unfortunately, there have been instances where debunking has been misapplied or questionably applied. When it is not nobly inspired, debunking can lead to mediocre science by torpedoing new ideas worthy of science looking into. It is important to realize that earnest defenders of a view, its true believers, are not expected to be dispassionate, open-minded, honest, or nice. Rather, they're expected to be passionate, focused, loyal, and effective. This goes for any view, be it scientific or nonscientific.

Demarcation is the name given the basis for judging whether something is or is not to be regarded scientific. Even though the definition of science is a basis for making this judgment it is not sufficiently precise to always suffice, necessitating supplementary considerations. Harold Brown, a philosopher of science, studied what is referred to as the demarcation problem and concluded there was no criterion or set of criteria, as of 1977, that would eliminate mistakes when deciding whether such-and-such a view is scientific or nonscientific. An example he gives of a likely mistake was scientists branding as nonscientific and pseudoscientific the celestial cataclysm theory set forth by Immanuel Velikovsky in 1950 (Brown, 1977, pp 160-164). This was a sad tale of impugning and lampooning unbecoming to scientists. Another instance of this kind of injustice was the negative attitude of scientists toward the remote-viewing (paranormal/psychic) research done in the mid and late 1970s at the Stanford Research Institute by two of its physicists, Hal Puthoff and Russell Targ.

The CSICP is a vehicle for airing opinions of people concerned about unorthodox views of any kind, especially views labeled pseudoscientific. Its chief publication is the Skeptical Inquirer. Since 2000, some of its members have even written articles that are critical of religious views. This is to be expected, being that many of its members are self-proclaimed modern humanists and thus not favorably disposed toward religion (page 30). Different in orientation from The Committee for the Scientific Investigation of Claims of the Paranormal is the Society for Scientific Exploration. It supports scientific research on what are known as anomalies (anomalous phenomena) and reports the findings of this research in its Journal of Scientific Exploration. Also different from the CSICP was The Sourcebook Project, begun by William Corlis around 1973. It existed until his death in 2011. Corliss rounded up thousands of published articles on anomalies and reproduced them in a bimonthly newsletter, Science Frontiers, and in more than a dozen thick Handbooks.

It is tempting to speculate upon a connection between the debunking by accepted science of certain views it labels nonscientific, particularly when done relentlessly, and the occurrence of revolutions within certain sciences. According to American physicist Thomas Kuhn, a mature science (e.g., biology) normally possesses an overall conceptual framework which dictates what is acceptable to it insofar as views, terminology, things observed, techniques used, and research problems formulated. This overall conceptual framework is the accepted image of said science (accepted biology) and guides the thinking and activities of the science's practitioners (biologists) for a long time, from a half century to a century or so. An overall conceptual framework constitutes normal science (normal biology), being that it is what's normal for a science during the time the science is under its sway.

Every once in a while, says Kuhn, anomalies discovered by a science pile up to the point its overall conceptual framework no longer appears viable. When that point is reached, the science is ripe for a change in its (overall conceptual) framework. If an apparently better framework comes along after this point is reached, then it will replace the old one. The transition from old to new frameworks happens fairly fast, within say twenty years. During the time it is taking place the science in question is said to be undergoing what Kuhn terms a scientific revolution. Now revolution is apropos, given the enormity of changes made and the unnerving effect these changes have on scientists in the science experiencing them. Physics had a scientific revolution in the early 1900s. It was triggered by the births of quantum theory and relativity theory. American physicist George Gamow recounted the ensuing changes and trauma in physics caused by quantum theory in his book Thirty Years That Shook Physics.

References

Brown, Harold I. Perception, Theory and Commitment: The New Philosophy of Science Chicago: University of Chicago Press, 1977 (hard). Pages cited in the chapter are part of a fine account on demarcation, the basis for judging whether something is or isn't to be accepted as scientific.

Cavendish, Richard A History Of Magic. New York: Taplinger, 1979 (fairly easy). An erudite account of not only magic but neo-Platonism, Pythagoreanism, Hermeticism, etc. All have to varying degrees been troublesome for science, and religion.

Ferngren, Gary B. (Editor) Science & Religion: A Historical Introduction. Baltimore: The Johns Hopkins University Press, 2002 (fairly easy). Presents diverse glimpses at relations between science and religion as well as at scientific ideas, mainly from medieval times until now.

Frazier, Kendrick UFOs, horoscopes, Bigfoot, psychics, and other nonsense. Smithsonian, 1978, March, 55-60.

Gardner, Martin Fads & Fallacies In The Name Of Science. New York: Dover, 1957 (easy). A classic look at pseudoscience up to 1957 which still is informative.

Korey, Kenneth The Essential Darwin: Selections And Commentary. Boston: Little, Brown and Company, 1984 (fairly easy). An excellent study of Darwin's theory from the mid 1830s up to the mid 1980s.

Ross, Hugh Beyond The Cosmos. Colorado Springs: NAVPRESS, 1996 (fairly hard). An interesting perspective on science and religion by someone steeped in both.

Taylor, Sherwood F. A Short History Of Science & Scientific Thought. New York: W.W. Norton, 1963.

CHAPTER 5

Science And Society

During the time natural philosophy evolved into reformed natural philosophy (1600-1800), it gradually went from being a social activity in one and then another of Europe's modernizing nations towards being a European social institution, which it became about 1850. Reformed natural philosophy commenced being called modern science, or simply science, around 1875. Now while reformed natural philosophy/science was still just an activity in Europe it had an impact on European culture, its impact taking the form of the heliocentric view (page 50), determinism/causation (page 8), and materialism (page 9). But upon becoming a social institution, science started to exert a lot more influence on Europe. And as of 1925 its impact was being felt throughout the world: America, Japan, India, Turkey, Mexico, etc.

This chapter looks at science after it became a social institution. We will discuss first the effect of science on society and next the effect of society on science. Sometimes the effect of science on society has been on another social institution: the family, education, religion, technology, medicine, government, politics, or the economy. But usually, its influence has been on society as a whole.

One influence of science on society began in 1859. It was a scientific view about the origin of life set forth by Darwin and called Darwin's theory of biological evolution, or simply Darwinism. Inasmuch as Darwinism is contrary so how the Bible says all life came to be, created by God in six days, it was denounced by Christians; principally by the clergy, since parishioners knew little about Darwinism until after 1900. This attack was seen by some scientists (Christian, non-Christian, atheist, and agnostic alike) as an attack on not only Darwin and his theory but science itself. Which led them to be wary of Christian religion. Scientists still remembered Galileo's trouble with the Inquisition and papacy as well as of Copernicus, Descartes, and Kepler worrying about running afoul of the Catholic Church.

Now by about 1900 a kind of truce had been reached in Europe between science and most Christian sects. Not so in America, because American Christians were generally more conservative than European Christians. This is evidenced by where Protestant fundamentalism, a type of conservative Christianity, sprang up and what it stands for. It originated in America in World War I. Fundamentalism's purpose was to reverse the liberal trend in American Christianity which had surfaced after the Civil War by insisting that a literal interpretation of the Bible be fundamental (hence, fundamentalism) to Christian living and teaching (therefore its concern with public education). The rise of modern humanism during the mid 1920s, also in America, was partly a reaction to attacks on scientific views by fundamentalists during the 1920s. Modern humanism (page 30) is what conservative Christians deride as secular humanism. Secular means worldly. To a conservative Christian worldly doesn't mean knowing the world and its people. Rather, it means materialistic, self-serving values contrary to Christian family-based values. As of 2025, no truce is in sight in America between science and the conservative sects of Christianity.

In the mid and late 1800s there were breakthroughs in basic physics and chemistry. They resulted in the creation of applied physics and chemistry. Applied physics led to the creation of thermodynamic and electrical engineering while applied chemistry led to the creation of chemical engineering and to improvements in medicine and public health. There've been strong ties between applied science and engineering technology ever since, as clearly seen in product research and development (R & D). The hand-in-glove relationship between the two often makes it difficult to tell them apart. This relationship is such that if engineering runs into a roadblock then applied physics or chemistry helps solve the problem by bringing to bear its insights on the latest knowledge of basic physics or chemistry. Many things invented in the mid and late

1800s owed their existence to science, either directly (applied science) or indirectly (technology).

Even though the power of steam had been harnessed well enough by 1800 to permit steam-powered water pumps (for removing water from coal mines), these steam engines were, for their size, inefficient. Not until thermodynamic engineering in the mid 1800s made steam engines more efficient would steamships and steam locomotives appear that would revolutionize transporting people, merchandise, and raw materials. Steam shovels and steam-powered logging equipment appeared during the late 1800s. The advents of the electric motor (1835), a better dynamo for generating electricity (1865), and the light bulb (1880) paved the way for the electrification of factories during the late 1860s and thus for industry having electrically powered machines and electric lighting. By 1900, electric utility companies were being formed to build and run power plants for supplying cities followed by towns with electricity. Electric elevators with adequate safety guards (1855), which are automatically activated when an elevator cable snaps, made it practical to construct buildings taller than five stories. Also made possible by electricity was telecommunication in the forms of the telegraph (1845) and telephone (1875).

Ways to mass-produce compounds (i.e., atoms of two or more chemical elements held together by the atoms' electrons) ushered in the large-scale transformation of raw materials into refined materials. Mills manufactured steel from iron ore (1860) and the first alloy steels, or steel alloys (1885). Structural steel girders enabled buildings to be a great deal taller than five stories, leading about 1890 to buildings so high they scraped the sky. Refining petroleum, or oil, using facilities aptly termed petroleum refineries began during the late 1800s and led to mass production of petroleum and petroleum products (e.g., gasoline). This and efficient gasoline-powered internal combustion engines (1885) made automobiles a reality in the 1890s. Synthetic dyes (1850) gave rise, among many other things, to staining techniques for identifying strains, or species, of bacteria (1885). Rayon, the first synthetic fiber, was invented in 1890. In approximately 1865, the process known as pasteurization was applied to prolonging the life of bottled wine and beer and, eventually, to rendering milk safer. The late 1800s saw headway made in preventing and treating such diseases as anthrax in livestock (1880), rabies in humans (1885), and diphtheria (1890).

Though these inventions benefited society, they benefited science too. For society thanked science by admiring it and by urging citizens to know more about it from the books and lectures of science's popularizers (e.g., Friedrich Humboldt, John Tyndall, Thomas Huxley, etc.). And capitalists born of the Industrial Revolution saw in science, mainly applied science, means to their end and responded by investing in and defending (applied) science. Which meant scientific research was now guided by not only theory, as in basic science, but business/corporate projects enlisting the aid of applied science (page 32). It also meant that pragmatic business-oriented scientists (applied scientists) were now joining the ranks of what before 1850 had been basic scientists. The public became aware of science's interest in nature and its role in technological innovation! Discovery of stars, galaxies, a new planet, and Martian 'canals'; a closer look at Saturn's rings; exploring caverns; unearthing the skull of Neanderthal man and the fabled city of Troy; learning about the Maya and more about the ancient Egyptians: many people found such tidbits of knowledge, along with the aforementioned inventions, to be exciting. In the late 1800s their excitement inspired a new genre in literature called science fiction, Robert Louis Stevenson and H. G. Wells being its first famous authors, and inspired world fairs (international expositions) like those held in Paris and Chicago, at which the latest technological marvels were showcased.

Darwin's theory inspired two developments in the late 1800s, social Darwinism and eugenics. Social Darwinism is a blend of social and political ideology which justifies one group of people (e.g., whites) dominating another group of people (e.g., blacks). Its justification is a perversion of ideas in Darwin's theory and in a theory of human social evolution constructed in the 1850s by English social philosopher/ social scientist Herbert Spencer. Darwin said only species having the right (states of the right) characteristics survive. Spencer said only groups of people with the right characteristics survive, it being he who is responsible for the expression 'survival of the fittest'. Neither Darwin nor Spencer were chauvinists, individuals who think they are superior to others. But their theories and their prestige were misused by individuals who were chauvinists, the social Darwinists.

Eugenics is an offshoot of social Darwinism. It was invented by Francis Galton, an English anthropologist. Eugenics has two goals. One is to study how a nation can improve the biological and particularly the mental characteristics of its citizens. The other is to create a social program designed to assure the biological and mental fitness of a country's citizenry. Both goals are implemented by selectively altering the inheritance of human characteristics and thereby increasing the inheritance of desirable characteristics and decreasing the inheritance of undesirable characteristics. Hence the aim of eugenics is to override natural selection (selection done by nature) and replace it with artificial selection (selection done by people). Of course, this is not something new. Artificial selection of plants and animals has been done for centuries by gardeners, farmers, and herders who cross-pollinate plants and cross-breed animals to (artificially) create strains of plants and breeds of animals exhibiting certain states of certain characteristics that are thought desirable, either for their beauty (e.g., pretty color or sleek lines) or their utility (e.g., high-yielding or sturdy). But what is new with eugenics is using artificial selection to reengineer humans, not animals and plants, as well as utilizing more drastic measures to eradicate perceived inferiority.

Social Darwinism and eugenics had a following in England and America from 1890 into the early 1940s, when their popularity plummeted. The sudden loss in their appeal was due to people inclined toward them not wanting to be seen condoning the appalling events in Germany during World War II, where Nazis attempted to preserve the so-called Aryan race they prided themselves belonging to by sterilizing and exterminating literally millions of Jews, Gypsies, and others they deemed undesirable, inferior, of poor stock, or tainted by questionable bloodlines (bloodline is another name for family tree or line of inheritance, it once being thought that what people inherit is carried in the blood of their parents). Eugenics and concerns over alleged racial purity intensified in southeastern Europe and parts of Africa during the 1990s. As of 2025, there are Americans who hate minorities and are, at heart, social Darwinists and eugenicists. Among them are people who think ethnic cleansing (genocide) is notall that bad.

Besides social Darwinism and eugenics, Darwinism heightened interest in knowing to what degree human mental characteristics and behavior are caused/determined by heredity or by environment. This interest came to include more advanced animals, particularly apes. Out of it came the nature-nurture, heredity-environment, orgenetic determinism-environmental determinism issue. The controversy became contentious in the mid 1900s when a few scientists took the extreme position that human mental characteristics and the mental processes giving rise to them are due totally to nature/heredity/genes. Also Darwinism sparked interest in observing the behavior of more advanced animals, especially apes. These observations were naturalistic and furnished the basis for describing animal behavior. Many scientists used their observations to explain animal behavior. Some of them explained animal behavior in terms of human mental processes, which, as we've seen, bothered Morgan (page 39), Watson (page 61), and Skinner (page 62).

From 1900 to 2000, science made great strides knowing about human inheritance. First, in 1900 the laws governing the inheritance of characteristics (the laws of heredity) became known. Second, in 1910 chromosomes inside the nucleus of the cell were identified as the carriers of inheritance factors termed genes, chromosomes having been discovered during the 1870s by employing a newly invented staining technique. Third, in 1910 it became known, too, that particular genes are located at particular points along chromosomes of fruit flies. Fourth, in 1929 deoxyribonucleic acid, or DNA, was found inside chromosomes. DNA is a compound that exists as a macromolecule, a molecule composed of hundreds of thousands of atoms. In 1944 the DNA molecule was shown to be that part of a chromosome which carries genes. This furnished the material basis for inheritance that Darwin's theory needed in order to win increased scientific acceptance, making Darwinists ecstatic. Fifth, in 1953 the structure of, or the arrangement of atoms within, DNA molecules was described. Every molecule consists of two strands. The two strands are normally wound round each other, giving them the appearance of a double helix (spiral or coil).

Sixth, during the 1960s there began a selective process of mapping (identifying) the precise sites (locations) of certain genes of interest on chromosomes in nuclei of cells in humans and in certain animals and plants. The primary purpose was to learn more about specific illnesses and medical conditions so as to devise more effective ways of treating or preventing them. Seventh, in the early 1970s a technique was invented enabling us to rearrange the genes in a DNA molecule and thus to recombine DNA. This 'recombinant DNA' was initially hailed as a wonderful accomplishment. However, it was soon dreaded by many. A more enlightened assessment of recombinant DNA surfaced during the late 1970s. Finally, around 2002, all 35,000 genes within the nucleus of every human cell and the sites of these genes on a cell's 46 chromosomes (23 supplied by each parent) became known, thanks to an immense undertaking begun in the late 1980s called the Human Genome Project. Genome means all genes in all cells of a certain species. Some people likened learning the human genome to discovering the Holy Grail; others likened it to opening Pandora's box.

My reference to Pandora's box stems from reflecting upon the consequences of the vast gulf which has come to separate our moral progress and our technological progress since around 1800. Consider an analogy. In 1800, we had such-and-such as an average level of morality and were able to use the sparks from a flint striking a metal lock plate to ignite the black gunpowder inside the barrel of a musket. In 1900, we had on average the same level of morality and could use electricity flowing through wires, from a battery to a stick of dynamite, to ignite the dynamite. And in 2000 we, still with the same level of morality as in 1800, were able to use waves flowing through air, from a radio transmitter to a radio receiver, to trigger a nuclear device. This steadily growing mismatch between our morality and our technology cannot go on forever, since it is self-limiting. Hence there exists a feedback loop between them that, after a specific level of mismatch occurs, will automatically correct this error- right this wrong - by either increasing our morality or decreasing our technology. In other words, the misuse of technology will cause things to happen (e.g., nuclear meltdowns or global warming) that undermine the socioeconomic systems perpetuating this mismatch.

On page 69 we saw the emergence of three new forms of technology (engineering) from the applied physics and applied chemistry which had emerged from basic physics and basic chemistry: thermodynamic engineering (1830), chemical engineering (1840), and electrical engineering (1880). They joined older forms of technology, like civil engineering (3000 B.C.), mining engineering (1500), mechanical engineering (1600), and hydraulic engineering (1700). And they would, in turn, be joined during the early and mid 1900s by such new forms as communications engineering (1900), an outgrowth of electrical engineering; aeronautical engineering (1910); control engineering (1920); industrial engineering (1930); operations research/management science (1940); computer engineering/science (1945); nuclear engineering/technology (1945); space technology (1955); ergonomics/human engineering (1955), which refers to designing sophisticated man-machine systems or systems where a human and the machine that he/she operates need to interface, or mesh, very well; fiber optics technology (1960); and biomedical engineering/technology (1960). From biomedical technology came genetic engineering (1972). Its debut was signaled by birth of a strain of virus hitherto unknown to nature, because it was made by recombining the DNA in an existing virus.

Scientifically speaking, the 1900s was a time of progressively reducing explanations of things and relationships (between characteristics of things) to things making them up. Put another way, it was a time of progress in what on page 10 (item 4) were termed causal reductionistic explanations. An instance of such reductionism is the explanatory knowledge generated about us and other animals in our taxonomic class, mammals. In 1900, we, and they, were usually explained in terms of our bodily systems (e.g., our skeletal, digestive, and visual systems) or the organs in them (e.g., our stomach, intestines, eyes, and brain). In 1920, these systems and organs were usually explained in terms of tissues (i.e., sheets or clusters of cells of a particular type) comprising them and consequently we, too, were explained in tissue terms. In 1940, our tissues (e.g., nerves, muscles, and skin) were usually explained in reference to specific cells constituting them (e.g., nerve cells, muscle cells, and skin cells) and so we were also explained in cell terms. In 1960, our cells (e.g., nerve cells) were usually explained in reference to their major components (i.e., axons, synaptic vesicles, mitochondria, chromosomes, etc.) and we were likewise explained in reference to cellular components. Finally, in 1980, the major components of our cells were usually explained in terms of the molecular compounds making them up, as were we.

We therefore went in less than a century from the level of organization of systems, down through the level of organization of an estimated 100 trillion cells comprising our bodies, to the level of organization of the billions of atoms making up a single human cell. How people in 1980 thought about their bodies is thus bound to differ from how people in 1900 thought about their bodies (assuming they knew what biology knew in 1980 and 1900).

Technologically speaking, the 1900s saw an explosion in achievements. A partial list of them includes airplanes, rockets, manned space capsules, trips to the moon, unmanned space probes to planets, orbiting weather and communication satellites, space stations used as laboratories/observatories, scuba (self-contained underwater breathing apparatus) gear, undersea laboratories, motion pictures, broadcasting stations, radio and television sets, two-way radios, microwave communications and ovens, radar and sonar equipment, hydroelectric and nuclear power plants, acrylic sheets (e.g., Plexiglas) and fibers (e.g., Orlon), nylon, disinfectants, medical diagnostic procedures (from tests for diabetes to full-body scans), hearing aids, medicines, vaccines (against typhoid fever, polio, influenza, pneumonia, etc.), prostheses (e.g., artificial knees, hips, and limbs), heart pacemakers, dialysis machines, fertilizers, pesticides, food preservatives, electro-mechanical followed by electronic cash registers and calculators, cell phones, and the internet. Many accomplishments resulted from progressively reducing the size of their components: from large vacuum tubes to small transistors, from circuits to integrated circuits ('chips', because they are on silicon chips) to subminiature circuits (microchips), and from mainframe computers occupying huge rooms to personal computers (PCs) on desks to laptop (lap-size) computers to even smaller microprocessors used in controlling processes (in automobile ignitions, pipelines, and electric power grids). And about 1995 nanotechnology commenced developing molecular machines so small they are essentially invisible to the naked eye.

The social impact of technological advances is complex and still being fathomed. A rough guess is that much of what we have done since 1900 has led us to today's grave social dilemma. Our dilemma is that by successfully applying knowledge about how to decrease infertility, decrease infant mortality, and increase longevity we are increasing the number of people competing for shrinking resources, increasing pollution of all sorts, and decreasing habitable space on earth for us and other lives. One solution toyed with is to establish colonies on immense space stations or on 'terra-formed' planets or moons. Yet even if this were possible, we might find that intelligent life elsewhere in the universe has systematically observed us long enough to decide it will not let us damage the rest of the universe like we have damaged earth. The warning issued by Klaatu at the end of the thought-provoking science fiction movie The Day The Earth Stood Still is today as timely as it was when the movie was first released in 1951.

Speaking of intelligent life elsewhere in the universe, during the 1970s America launched four unmanned interplanetary space probes containing, among other things, information for any extraterrestrials (ETs) that might happen upon them (Sagan, 1978). Pioneers 10 and 11 were launched in 1971 and 1972. Voyagers 1 and 2 were launched in 1977. Each Pioneer had a plaque attached to a strut supporting one of its antennae, The plaque had drawings of a man and woman standing side-by-side, our solar system, and our planet. Each Voyager had attached to its hull a phonograph record, stylus, and instructions on how to play the record. The record had greetings in 55 languages, music from around the world, and 116 acoustically encoded photographs of people and earth. Nobody knows if any ET's have seen them.

With the onset of the Scientific Revolution there commenced a steady growth in the magnifying power of telescopes employed by astronomers. The result was a steady increase in new things observed in the night sky. Some of them were stars not seen using weaker telescopes. Others were nebulas (i.e., immense clouds of luminous gas and dust) and galaxies (i.e., enormous clusters of millions of stars). Our sun and solar system are in the Milky Way galaxy, half-way out from its center. Careful study of newly observed stars indicated they are further from us than earlier observed stars. This was contrary to what the theories of Aristotle, Ptolemy, and Copernicus said; namely, stars are imbedded in the outermost celestial sphere. Their theories implied two things. One is that all stars are the same distance from earth, not different distances from earth. The other is that the size of the universe is limited, not limitless. In 1960, after 300 years of observing more and more new stars further and further from earth, astronomers began to think that the universe is not only limitless but expanding.

Between 1885 and 1915, the public was intrigued with earth's neighboring planet Mars, occasionally called the red planet due to the redness of the iron oxide on its surface. The public's intrigue resulted from the findings of a few astronomers in the late 1800s. Now as Mars and earth travel along their orbits they progressively move closer to and then further away from each other. Astronomers wanting to know the surface features of Mars observe the planet when it and earth are relatively close. Every 32 years, the two are closest. They were closest in 1830, 1862, and 1894. In 1830 and 1862, a few astronomers drew detailed maps of the Martian surface. And in 1877, a year that Mars and earth were closer than normal but not closest, the Italian astronomer Giovanni Schiaparelli created a very detailed map of the Martian landscape. On it he drew a network of thin straight lines he observed on the surface of Mars, lines that he hypothesized to be channels (canali in Italian). Schiaparelli didn't venture a guess on whether they were due to nature (e.g., water erosion) or Martians.

When Schiaparelli's map was translated into English, its word canali was called canals. This was a big mistake. For channel means a work of nature while canal signifies a work of man. Therefore, calling the channels canals implied they were made by Martians. Needless to say, the map's English version caused a stir inside and outside the scientific community and embarrassment for Schiaparelli. The 'canals', along with previously observed polar ice caps and previously observed changes in color of certain areas which suggested seasonal changes in 'vegetation', painted a captivating picture of Mars teeming with advanced forms of life. Two astronomers, the Frenchman Nicolas Flammarion and the American Percival Lowell, added more details to and championed this image of Mars while English novelist H. G. Wells told in his book The War Of The Worlds a story about earth's invasion by Martians looking for a new home. By 1915, the opinion of most astronomers was that the canals, channels, or lines are optical illusions and that Mars has no life. Scientific opinion remains unchanged after analyzing data telemetered from space probes and robotic land rovers.

Curiosity, imagination, patience, and an open mind are good qualities in a scientist. So is restraint. Lack of restraint by Flammarion and Lowell led to their colleagues being perturbed with them, not only for acting like their unconfirmed hypotheses were confirmed but stating or intimating to the public their hypotheses were well confirmed. They were seen as confusing science fiction with science fact and thereby sullying the name of science. By 1900, scientists had begun being concerned about the public's perception of science. The reason was the anger over geological and particularly biological evolution being vented by a rising tide conservative Christians. And as of 1900 biologists did not yet have a material basis for justifying Darwinism and thus were reluctant to defend it in the public arena. Furthermore, scientists saw on the horizon potential problems posed by the new science of psychology, chiefly it embracing nonmaterialism (page 9, item 2) and indeterminism/free-will (page 24). This is why many scientists were slow to accept psychology as a science. Some still don't feel it is a science.

In 1900, scientists were concerned, too, with the recent appearance of pseudoscience masquerading as science. One pseudoscientific belief was the existence of the now submerged continents of Atlantis and Lemuria. They are elements in an intricate worldview promulgated by Theosophy. Theosophy arose in the 1870s as an alternative to Christian religion and modern science. By 1900, it was a thorn in the sides of both. To extend what American astronomer Carl Sagan once said in regard to claims that extraterrestrials exist, we can say that all extraordinary claims, be they the existence of extraterrestrials or of Atlantis and Lemuria, ought to be accepted only when there is extraordinary evidence (clearly compelling evidence) to back these claims.

Absence of compelling evidence is the reason an hypothesis created in 1912 by the German meteorologist-geologist Alfred Wegener about a continent that no longer exists was given the cold shoulder by scientists. Wegener, like some before him, was baffled by the shapes of the west coast of Africa and east coast of South America as well as by similarities between the two continents insofar as their geological formations, animal life, and plant life. His hypothesis explained these things by saying earth's surface began as one gigantic continent (Pangaea, meaning All-earth) and one gigantic ocean (Panthalassa, meaning All-sea) and that roughly 235 million years ago the continent started splitting into smaller continents, which drifted ever so slowly apart until reaching their present locations. As with Darwin's theory before genes were viewed as tiny segments along the two strands making up a DNA molecule and as with Kepler's heliocentric theory before the advent of Newton's universal gravitation hypothesis (page 23), Wegener's continental drift hypothesis lacked the material basis needed for scientists to feel comfortable accepting it. Consequently, most scientists regarded it nonscientific and akin to Atlantis, Lemuria, and Martians. That all changed in the 1960s after finding a material basis for it in tectonic forces, lithospheric plates, seafloor spreading, subduction zones, etc. By 1970, his continental drift hypothesis had been recast as the theory of plate tectonics and had acquired broad scientific support.

Nearly all scientists distanced themselves from the topic of UFOs, or unidentified flying objects, after these frequently saucer-shape enigmas began, from the mid 1950s onward, to be also tied to other enigmas, like contacts (e.g., by George Adamski) with their occupants, abductions (e.g., of Barney and Betty Hill) by their occupants, men in black (MIBs), flying creatures ('mothmen'), livestock mutilations, and crop circles. It turns out that UFOs and UFO-related phenomena have been reported for centuries and thus are not new. However, widespread public awareness of them was new, thanks to newspaper reports starting in 1947 of sightings and to books by investigative reporters, beginning about 1965, on contacts/abductions. Typically, one or more UFOs have been spotted by one, two, or a few individuals. On rare occasions a fairly large area has been inundated for days or weeks by sightings, something termed a flap. Typically, too, contacts and abductions have been difficult to corroborate. Some reports reflect what really happened, or as usually put, what individual(s) believed happened, which is the best way to characterize such reports. Others have been shown to be bogus.

The disturbing thing about all of this is the phenomenon's unpredictability and thus our inability, after more than sixty years of trying, to go from observing it unsystematically to observing it systematically. One is tempted to say the phenomenon has a mind of its own and deliberately thwarts our efforts to know it better by feeding us incomplete or inconsistent information about itself. Inability to know more about UFOs and related phenomena led some governments and scientists around the world to begin minimizing them in the 1950s and debunking them in the 1960s. This led to charges of government cover-ups and disinformation campaigns (later found true of the U.S. government) and to the creation of unyielding true believers and unyielding true disbelievers.

A few scientists have studied the global evidence and concluded, frequently to the detriment of their standing within the scientific community, that the evidence suggests the existence of unknown intelligences of unknown origin. Said scientists have included the American astronomer J. Allen Hynek, French astronomer and computer scientist Jacques Vallee, and American physicist Stanton Friedman. The UFO origins that have been entertained include outer space (extraterrestrials), dimension(s) in addition to the four of space-time (ultraterrestrials), and earth. I will not here venture further into this minefield but will in the next chapter. Suffice it to say, there is a lot more to UFOs and UFO-related phenomena than meets the eye.

As the 1900s unfolded, public interest in physics reached that of astronomy during the late 1800s. One reason for this was physics inserting some of itself into astronomy during the late 1800s and creating the interdisciplinary-hybrid-science of astrophysics, much like it about the same time allied aspects of itself with chemistry (creating physical chemistry), geology (creating geophysics), and psychology (creating psychophysics) and like it around 1850 had grafted part of itself onto biology (creating biophysics). These unions were good and doubly good for physics, since it could, without mustering much effort, share in the many successes it made possible for biology, astronomy, chemistry, geology, and psychology. This is not to say that during the 1900s physics rested on its laurels or rode on the coattails of hybrids it helped create. In the 1900s, physics made important theoretical breakthroughs that, when popularized, found an interested public. Naturally a layperson seldom came to understand theories of physics the way physicists do. But that's beside the point. The point is a person often finished reading a popular book or magazine article on these theories feeling he/she knew them well enough to understand nature a little better than previously.

It will be sufficient to say only a few words about the theoretical advances made by physics during the 1900s. The first of them was the theory of the quantum set forth in 1900 by German physicist Max Planck, a quantum being a tiny bundle (later a particle, called a photon) of energy. The next was relativity theory, devised by the American physicist Albert Einstein. It had two forms, the special theory of relativity (1905) and the general theory of relativity (1915). Quantum theory and relativity theory extended significantly relationships involving the characteristics motion and force, which until then had been the sole domain of Newton's law of universal gravitation, and in so doing they triggered a scientific revolution in physics which rocked physics from 1900 to 1930 (page 66).

Around 1925 quantum theory underwent overhauling. From 'old quantum theory' emerged 'quantum mechanics', the new quantum theory. Quantum mechanics has two faces. It is a theory explaining an atom's emission and absorption of energy in terms of its electrons emitting and absorbing photons (quanta). But, more fundamentally, it is that branch of physics which studies the motions of subatomic particles and the forces/energies inside atoms. Quantum mechanics is the home of such concepts as the French physicist Louis de Broglie's wavelike behavior of subatomic particles (1923), Austrian physicist Wolfgang Pauli's exclusion principle (1925), Danish physicist Niels Bohr's complementarity principle (1927), and German physicist Werner Heisenberg's uncertainty principle (1927).

A breather came in the mid 1900s. Then, in the 1970s, an hypothesis commenced being framed to explain a variety of hitherto inexplicable observations (e.g., hurricanes, the giant red spot on Jupiter, and airfoil turbulence) encountered by a variety of pursuits (meteorology, astronomy, and aeronautical engineering). The thing these observations have in common is they give the impression of chaotic relationships, or chaos. Hence, as the hypothesis was confirmed enough to be deemed a theory, around 1980, it started to go by the name chaos theory. In a chaotic relationship, its effect is not merely dependent upon its cause(s) but very sensitive to slight differences in its initial conditions [i.e., the initial state(s) manifested by the characteristic(s) that are the effect's cause(s)]. Said relationships are nonlinear or, more precisely, exponential. This means a plot on ordinary graph paper of the effect versus the initial conditions will lead to a rapidly rising curved line, instead of a rapidly rising straight line, which describes, say, a rapidly developing storm system (e.g., a tornado).

The last theoretical advance in physics during the 1900s was string theory. String theory, now discredited, started out in the late 1960s with the idea of a string. This idea was gradually refined throughout the 1970s and in about 1980 was made the basis for an hypothesis on strings. Around 1985 the string hypothesis came to be regarded a theory about strings. Two concepts are key to string theory. One is that space is more than the three dimensions we commonly acknowledge. Each of these other spatial dimensions is termed an extra dimension (of space). String theory usually treats space-time as a ten dimensional concept, all dimensions except time being dimensions of space. The other key concept is string, not a string in the ordinary sense of the word. Strings are theorized to be the origin of all types of subatomic particles and of the four kinds of fundamental forces inside an atom (which in order of increasing strength are the gravitational, weak nuclear, electromagnetic, and strong nuclear forces). Nature is conceived to consist of innumerable strings each of which, at any given location along the dimension of time, oscillates (vibrates) at specific frequencies (rates) at specific locations along specific extra dimensions. If the rate of a string's oscillation along one or more extra dimensions changes, then the string changes from one into another type of subatomic particle and/or from one into another kind of fundamental force.

Our discussion of science's effect on society has covered its influence via basic science, applied science, and technology/engineering. My final remark on the subject before discussing society's effect on science is summed up by the saying 'imitation is the sincerest form of flattery'. This seems true in regard to what people say and what people do.

First, many people outside science (and engineering/technology) imitate what scientists (and engineers/technologists) say. They may do it appropriately in order to convey information at a level of precision dictated by the situation at hand. Or they may do it inappropriately, to impress. Examples of scientific terminology popularly used outside the context of science during the past hundred years include: black hole, 'survival of the fittest', libido, scientific, (Thomas Kuhn's) paradigm shift, input, feedback, hypnotic, talking a quantum leap, clone, experiment, psycho (psychotic), quasar, fallout, random sample, the big bang (a theory in astronomy), and (mental) inertia. Second, some people outside science imitate what scientists do. By this I mean they do research using one or another method they think scientists use. Usually their methods are very similar to the method of science and typically produce good, applied knowledge. Yet strictly speaking, their methods are not the scientific method. The reason why is that their methods entail research but not (the integrated utilization of) *research and theory*.

The second interaction between science and society to be discussed is the influence of society on science. Basically, society has had two effects on science. One was the "counterculture movement', known simply as "the movement. It arose in America in about 1962.

Individuals making up the movement, primarily twenty to thirty years old, saw themselves as the instruments of social and political change and as pitted against 'the establishment', which stood for the status quo and therefore no sociopolitical change. The clash between the two groups has been characterized as a sociopolitical altercation between "liberals" (the movement) and 'conservatives" (the establishment). As the battles between them intensified during the mid and especially late 1960s, science got caught up in the fray. How come? Because it is a social institution. This indicates that its views are institutionalized, which is implied by the labels established, accepted, mainstream, and orthodox science (page 64). Science, meaning established science, was one out of many targets of the movement, a largely minor target. The major battlefields from 1962 to 1977 were racial equality, women's rights, legalizing marijuana, the rights of homosexuals, environmental protection, animal rights, organically grown foods, less restrictive sex, etc. Now the glue holding these diverse goals together as a movement was opposition to the controversial Vietnam War (1965-1973). So, when it ended, the movement, as such, collapsed. However, groups once embodying it continued fighting for their causes. Most of the groups are still with us, showing how durable the rift has been between liberal America and conservative America.

Let us now look at how the counterculture movement affected American science. Its influence included: funding multidisciplinary ecological research aimed at revealing the degrees, effects, and causes of environmental pollution; psychopharmacological research on the effects and addictiveness of marijuana and other mood-altering substances; biomedical research to identify safer, more effective, and less expensive birth control methods; sociological and anthropological research to learn if discrimination (based on gender, race, ethnicity, or sexual preference) is caused by stereotypes which arise from misinformation and disinformation intentionally released by social institutions (i.e., the establishment); and research geared to knowing altered states of consciousness better. Textbooks on earth science, biology, sociology, anthropology, and psychology published during the 1970s increasingly mentioned findings of research inspired by concerns of the counterculture.

The other influence society has had on science came in the form of a movement referred to as postmodernism and postmodern philosophy. Postmodernism arose in France about 1960, where it was popular from the mid 1960s until the late 1990s, and spread to England and America during the late 1970s. It was conceived by the French philosopher Michel Foucault. Foucault disliked reason and wanted to replace modern western civilization's rational approach to thinking with a new-postmodern-approach. His approach is difficult to understand, perhaps because it is irrational (the opposite of rational). Most of what can be understood about Foucault's philosophy are his specific gripes about rational thinking. There are four. First, language distorts all that we observe and our attitudes toward people, individually and collectively, as well as nature. Second, it is impossible to know the absolute truth about anything. Third, it is possible to know the relative truth about something, this being truth as known through the eye of its beholder. Fourth, it is consequently unjustifiable and wrong for authority figures (e.g., parents, teachers, ministers, and scientists) and social institutions (i.e., the family, education, religion, and science) to say they know (the truth about) the things they consider their realm of expertise (e.g., behaving responsibly, knowing history, knowing God, knowing nature). An offshoot of postmodernism called postmodern structuralism took root in France around 1970 and was also popular until the late 1990s. It was conceived by French philosopher Jacques Derrida, as was deconstruction.

Deconstruction means demonstrating how language makes it impossible for us to possess an intersubjectively verifiable (i.e., an objective) knowledge about anything.*

During the late 1960s in Europe and the 1980s in America, the members of a few women's rights/women's liberation groups began employing postmodernism/postmodern structuralism to further their social agendas. Such feminists as Luce Irigaray in Belgium and Katherine Hayles in America have accused science of reeking of male chauvinism (male superiority). They say men's inspirations and aspirations prevail in science and decree largely what science (physics being their big target) does research on and theorizes about. Irigaray and Hayles also criticize the way science conducts research and names concepts, its names of concepts often conjuring up images of the masculine ethos. The women's liberation movement has encouraged research characterized as feminist cultural studies.

In the mid 1970s, postmodernists commenced bandying scientific terms, mainly from physics. This they did when advocating their viewpoint and when attacking the credibility of society's institutions and what they saw as biased knowledge generated by the social sciences, especially psychology and sociology. Frequently the contexts in which they use scientific terms reveal their poor grasp, or no grasp at all, of what the terms mean, to what they pertain, or to what they can be validly applied. This is not surprising, since nothing they say can, from their relativistic standpoint, be legitimately deemed wrong. Numbered among the postmodernists are Jean-Francois Lyotard and Jean Baudrillard. Scientists getting wind of postmodern philosophy's misuse of their terminology got upset. They became more upset after fully realizing that their social institution was under siege by postmodernists.

A thing particularly troubling to scientists who've learned of it is a postmodernist development within the sociology of science (not to be confused with the philosophy of science). This development is called the strong programme in the sociology of science. It was conceived about 1980 by two Americans, Barry Barnes and David Bloor, as the means to attain their end of selling their belief that scientific knowledge be stated in terms of the causes in society for which this knowledge is the effect rather than, as has been the case ever since Aristotle, seeing scientific knowledge as causal relationships

---

*The remaining material in this chapter comes from a book by Sokal & Bricmont (1999).

in nature. The programme started to be championed in France during the late 1980s by Bruno Latour. It is unlikely that the strong program will rule the roost in science and thereby dictate what science is. Yet if this were to happen then the result would be a revolution in science which would make the Scientific Revolution look pale in comparison. In fact, it would doubtless be seen by mainstream scientists as what on page 8 was termed a foundation crisis, a crisis in science's foundation.

References

Barnes-Svarney, Patricia <u>The New York Public Library Science Desk Reference.</u> New York: Macmillan, 1995 (fairly hard). An excellent, still basically up-to-date synopsis of research and theoretical developments in natural science. Difficult things are discussed in a manner the novice will ordinarily find understandable.

Brookesmith, Peter <u>UFO: The Government Files</u>. New York: Barnes & Noble, 1996 (fairly easy). A fine and detailed summary of much of what the American government knows about unidentified flying objects and phenomena related to them, made possible largely through a 1974 amendment to the Freedom of Information Act of 1966.

Good, Timothy <u>Earth: An Alien Enterprise</u>. New York: Pegasus Books, 2013 (fairly hard). Another fine and detailed summary of governmental obfuscation regarding UFOs, this one being more recent and much more detailed than Brookesmith's.

Jacoby, Russell and Glauberman, Naomi (Editors) <u>The Bell Curve Debate</u>. New York: Times Books, 1995 (fairly hard). This book is a compilation of dozens of professional's reactions to the allegedly scientific views in a book published merely a year before, The Bell Curve written by Richard Herrnstein (an experimental psychologist) and Charles Murray (a political scientist). Bell curve is the popular name for normal distribution, a probability distribution which looks like an old-fashioned church bell. Normal distributions are often used to describe by how much things (e.g., people) differ from each other in regard to the characteristics (e.g., IQ, or intelligence quotient) they possess. Put another way, bell curves frequently serve as models-descriptions- of dispersion in (the states manifested by) the characteristics of things. Now, Herrnstein and Murray's views lead them to conclude that our country should adopt public policies for dealing with citizens scoring below average on (traditional) intelligence tests. Such policies would avert what they saw as the imminent collapse of American society. Their book is a mixture of truths, half-truths, and falsities and reflects a growing 'conservative' sociopolitical climate in America during the late 1900s. One chapter in Jacoby and Glauberman's book, by Howard Gardner, is in my opinion a good assessment of The Bell Curve's scientific worth, which Gardner says is negligible at best. It may well be The Bell Curve is an example of scientists engaging in pseudoscience.

Kurzweil, Ray <u>The Singularity is Near</u>. New York: Penguin Group, 2005 (hard). A panoramic view of nanotechnology and an amazing forecast of where it will have led us by the year 2040.

Randall, Lisa <u>Warped Passages</u>. New York: Harper Collins Publishers, 2005 (fairly hard). This is a thorough discussion by a theoretical physicist of the latest ideas on dimensions besides the ones with which we're familiar and the reasons for invoking them. She makes these very abstract ideas as clear as they probably can be made.

Randle, Kevin D.; Estes, Russ; and Cone, William P. <u>The Abduction Enigma</u>. New York: Forge/Tom Doherty Associates, 1999 (fairly easy). Provides an assessment of reports of abductions by aliens (occupants of UFOs).

Sagan, Carl <u>Murmurs Of Earth</u>. New York: Random House, 1978 (easy). An excellent account of the thinking behind the information affixed to the hulls of the two Voyager interplanetary space probes launched by America in 1977, information intended for the edification of any extraterrestrials intercepting them.

Sokal, Alan D. and Bricmont, Jean <u>Fashionable Nonsense: Postmodern Intellectuals' Abuse of Science.</u> New York: Pacador (St. Martin's Press), 1999 (fairly easy). This is one of the few thorough examinations of pseudoscientific assertions in the literature of postmodern philosophy, assertions the public ought to be aware of.

CHAPTER 6

Looking To The Future

About 1830, French philosopher Auguste Comte, founder of the science sociology and the philosophy of science positivism, expressed the following sentiments:

"The evolution of the mind is in three stages - the theological, the metaphysical, and the positive. The theological is the stage of primitive culture, in which all events are explained by reference to the wills of personal beings. In the metaphysical stage, explanations are in terms of impersonal forces and general concepts. But in full maturity the mind discards both of these and thinks in terms only of phenomena and their mathematical correlations (positive stage)." (Avey, 1961, p 186)

Phenomena, here, means observables or things we can observe. And positive is another way to say positivism, a term Comte recommended that science adopt as a replacement for the term empiricism (page 4).

He wrote the above passage about thirty years after the reformation of natural philosophy had come to an end and around fifty years before natural philosophy started to go increasingly by the name science. His words exude a feeling of triumphal pride in how the human intellect has progressed over the millennia and optimism as to what lies ahead. My intent in the present chapter is to do what Comte did nearly two hundred years ago, look back at the past and then to the future. This chapter will be more speculative than previous chapters.

The 1500s and 1600s were the last century of renaissance times (1300 to 1600) and the first century of modern times (after 1600). Also they were a time of major changes in European society, religion, and philosophy. Changes in one interacted with and thus produced changes in one or both of the others. After eight centuries of being *the* form of Christianity in all of Europe except for its eastern portion, Roman Catholicism had to share the limelight with Protestantism. Protestantism, in turn, had to soon adjust to it not taking just one but many forms, the many Protestant denominations (sects) that emerged between 1500 and 1700. And after three centuries of being *the* form of philosophy in Catholic Europe, Aristotelian philosophy was replaced by a string of new philosophies. Ignorant of nearly all the world which lay beyond Europe, the Middle East, and north Africa, Europe suddenly learned from its adventuresome seafarers a lot more about the world: North America, South America, the rest of Africa, Indonesia, Asia, and the larger islands in the Pacific Ocean. These new lands were not mere places. They were places with people, animals, and plants that Europeans initially looked upon with awe and then as resources for satisfying their needs and desires, which soon led Europe to colonize and dominate much of the rest of the world for three centuries.

Aristotelian philosophy embraced Aristotle's thoughts on a wide variety of subjects, chiefly metaphysics, logic, rhetoric, morality, politics, astronomy, physics, and biology. His thoughts on astronomy, physics, and biology collectively constitute his natural philosophy. Aristotelian philosophy, Aristotelianism, was largely a rational philosophy, meaning it was largely based on using reason. The string of new philosophies which began to replace Aristotelian philosophy after 1600 were largely rational philosophies too, until philosophers started to lose interest in rationalism around 1800. Most of the philosophers contributing to the reformation of natural philosophy were empiricists. This makes sense, since it was individuals making systematic observations from 1300 onward that increasingly found discrepancies between what Aristotle said they will see and what they saw. The only rationalists involved in remaking natural philosophy were Descartes and the German philosopher Gottfried Leibniz.

Much happened in natural philosophy from 1800 to 1900. By 1800, its reformation was complete. Approximately 1850, reformed natural philosophy went from being an activity to being a social institution. In about 1875, (reformed) natural philosophy began to be increasingly called natural science and, eventually, science. Around 1875, definitions of science and the scientific method were set forth, most scientists accepting them by 1910. Finally, there were science's achievements between 1850 and 1900. We reviewed many of them on pages 69 through 72 in the last chapter. More occurred from 1900 to 2000, as seen on pages 73 through 81.

Where is science going? Theories give some indication since they guide research. Also, in a sense, research guides theories, research confirmations/disconfirmations of a theory occasionally indicating how the theory can be improved or even salvaged. It can even affect theories in another way. When money to fund research inspired by a theory drops or stops for whatever reason, the theory is no longer able to guide research aimed at either confirming/disconfirming it or describing it and thus it enters a state of suspended animation which if long enough results in the theory being forgotten.

Lots of money is spent on scientific research, whether performed in the name of basic science (e.g., elementary-particle research by physicists) or applied science (e.g., pharmacological research). It's research and not theory that makes science expensive, inasmuch as there are many, many more research scientists and their technicians and other support staff than there are theoretical scientists. Funds for financing scientific research vary from one fiscal budget-year to the next, as do priorities for doing this versus that specific type of scientific research. Both the funds and the priorities are determined by those with the money, who in America are principally the U.S. government and big businesses/corporations. Hence, despite theories offering some clue as to where science is headed, they are of little value hinting at what science will know or be doing five or ten years from now (2025).

Established/accepted/mainstream/orthodox science, meaning science, influences not only research funded but what textbooks and popular books on science are published, and ultimately what the public knows about science. Which is how (orthodox) science holds unorthodox science at bay. Unorthodox science is an activity that, unlike pseudoscience, employs the scientific method. Yet it is commonly said or intimated to be pseudoscience by scientists and science writers. The reason is to impugn the credibility of unorthodox scientists and thereby to prevent their theories and research findings from jeopardizing scientists' theories, research findings, and funding. As might be expected, sources for the funding of unorthodox research are scant. One source is the Society for Scientific Exploration mentioned on page 65.

Are there nonscientific views on nature which are scientifically interesting and can be formulated as testable hypotheses? I think there are. In what follows I discuss three broad groups of such views: UFOs and UFO-related phenomena, ancient legends/myths, and psychic phenomena. They could become part of what science finds itself doing in the foreseeable future.

1. UFOs and UFO-related phenomena

UFOs, or unidentified flying objects, and the phenomena related to them were encountered on pages 79 and 80. There are basically four UFO-related phenomena: humanoids (humanlike entities), human abductions, livestock mutilations, and crop circles. Much has been written concerning them. Below is a summary of what is publically known about UFOs and UFO-related phenomena.

UFOs come in various shapes and sizes. Before 1980, they were sometimes ball shape (e.g., the 'foo fighters' sighted in World War II and again during the Korean War) and five to ten feet in diameter. From 1947 onward, they were commonly disc/saucer shape and fifteen to fifty feet in diameter. Prevalent sightings of saucer-shape UFOs prompted the term 'flying saucers'. Cigar-shape vehicles 100 feet long and longer were increasingly observed after the 1960s. Since about 1980, small to medium-size diamond shapes have also been increasingly seen as well as huge V-shape craft spanning 300 to 600 feet, reminiscent of U.S. Air Force flying wing bombers of the late 1940s (although their wingspans were between 140 and 175 feet). On a clear day the balls, discs, and diamonds normally have a light gray, silvery appearance. At night they may emit no light or may have 'running lights' of varying color or may be entirely illuminated. UFOs have been reported to appear (materialize?) and disappear (dematerialize?) in a second. Frequently a UFO is not heard, even when close; sometimes it is heard making a humming sound or high-pitch sound. Since 1940, most have exhibited aeronautical performance far superior to that of contemporary U.S. fighter planes, like accelerating to thousands of mile per hour in a few seconds and making right-angle turns without slowing down. They emit intense electromagnetic radiation that interferes with electrical and particularly electronic circuits, which is why automobiles near a UFO often stop running until it moves on. Presumably all small UFOs, ones the size of foo fighters, are remotely controlled and therefore pilotless. Some among the larger (the more than 100-foot long) cigar-shape craft may be 'mother ships' which transport a dozen or so saucers, much as an aircraft carrier transports airplanes.

Humanoids have been observed in connection with UFOs since 1952. They are occasionally spotted outside a UFO that has landed, apparently working on it or collecting (soil, plant, insect, etc.) specimens, and are sometimes seen looking out of the windows of a UFO. Humanoids are always reported in human abductions. Differences in their physical appearance suggest there may be six or more species of humanoids presently 'visiting' earth. Two humanoid types predominate. One looks to varying degrees like us in height, weight, body build, skin color, hair color, and clothing worn. Members of this type communicate with us either in the language of the individual they contact or by means of telepathy. They communicate with each other in a language undecipherable to us or by telepathy. The other type of humanoid looks very different from us. Its members are called grays due to their typically pale gray, hairless skin. They stand three to four feet tall (though a few are five to eight feet tall); have thin bodies with big heads, no ears, no noses, and slits for mouths; have enormous black eyes without pupils; and wear snug, single-piece clothes that vaguely resemble a diver's wet suit. Grays communicate with us telepathically and with each other by 'chirping' sounds or by telepathy. Since 1965, more human contact has been with grays than with the first type of humanoid, at least this seems the case in America.

Most humanoid contacts with humans are more intimate than humans desire. This brings me to the phenomenon known as human abductions. Human abductions became a rapidly growing subdivision of human contacts with humanoids from 1965 onward as a growing number of human contactees also became human abductees. Yet the scope of human abductions was not known until 1970 and not well known until 1990, due to an abductee's fear of being laughed at, to an abductee repressing memories of the trauma of being abducted, or to amnesia imposed on abductees by their abductors. Many books have been written about human abductions by humanoids. Consequently, I am not able to get into more than the rudiments of human abduction.

Imagine two sequences of events. The first portrays an automobile with a driver and passenger traveling in broad daylight along a remote rural road. Ken, the passenger, tells the driver, Carol, about a light gray, silvery disc-shape object in the sky that he has been watching for a couple of minutes. He says that it is a few hundred feet above and a few hundred yards to the right of them. Carol suddenly has the urge to pull off the road and onto its breakdown strip. A minute later she loses consciousness and his consciousness begins fading. The second sequence of events portrays a husband, wife, and their three children (nine, ten, and twelve years old) living in a suburban house. It is 9:00 at night. The two younger children are asleep in their bedroom; the parents and oldest child are in the living room, the parents watching television while the child finishes homework on a computer. Their child complains that the computer is acting funny. A minute later the house lights flicker and then go out. In the darkness is seen a bright green light coming from outside the house into the living room, passing through spaces between the living room's closed venetian blinds. Amidst everyone's mounting concern, the husband and child become tired, sit down, and lose consciousness. The wife, Janet, wonders what is happening and then her consciousness fades. As you may now suspect, Ken in the first sequence and Janet in the second are in the process of being abducted.

What occurs next is pretty much the same for Ken and Janet. I'll describe the basic events and leave it to readers wanting more details to consult books cited in the chapter's References. An abductee floats on a beam of light to a landed or hovering UFO, passing effortlessly through intervening obstacles (e.g., ceilings, walls, closed doors). Once inside the UFO, the dazed abductee is escorted by humanoids, typically grays, to a room where samples of blood, flesh, sperms/eggs, etc. are obtained employing very technical looking equipment. This 'examination room' has multiple television-like screens flush with its walls which show changing, incomprehensible images. Enigmatic symbols are on instrument panels and occasionally on walls. Fairly often a tiny device is implanted beneath the skin, up the nose, etc. All the while the abductee is conscious but unable to move and aware yet not as anxious as one would expect, apparently because the humanoids have, by staring into the abductee's eyes, simultaneously paralyzed, anesthetized, and sedated him/her. Just before beaming an abductee back to his car/her house, he/she may be taken on a brief tour of the UFO. Once inside the car/house the abductee is exhausted, remembers nothing, and will sleep a lot during the next week or two. Ken/Janet feel that only a half-hour elapsed between their awareness fading and returning to normal when actually the time lapse was, say, three or four hours, a lapse in time ufologists (i.e., people who study UFOs) refer to as 'missing time'.

From 1965 onward, hypnotic sessions conducted by hypnotherapists unlocked the repressed and amnesia-imposed memories of more and more abductees and gave them necessary closure on their ordeals. The sessions revealed much, not all of it traumatic. An important finding was that many abductees emerged from their traumas imbued with a stronger character, improved abilities (some psychic), improved health (some ailments cured), a personal sense of duty to care for people and the earth, and renewed spirituality. It thus seems humanoid abductions of humans can have redeeming features.

Livestock mutilations have often been associated with UFO sightings. Therefore, some think ufonauts (humanoids) are behind them. Many mutilations of livestock have been reported since the late 1960s. Various body parts (e.g., eyes, ears, tongues, teeth, genitals, rectums, and udders) have been removed from animals in the fields in which they were grazing, removed with surgical precision sometimes exceeding that typically seen in well-equipped hospitals. No blood has been found on the ground where the carcasses lay and almost always the carcasses had been drained of blood. Some speculate that human abductions and livestock mutilations are part of a worldwide longitudinal, or long-term, program conducted by humanoids for monitoring changes in terrestrial things, meaning earth and all things (living and nonliving) on it. A few believe humanoids are utilizing earth as a R & D (research and development) center in order to make new things out of earth's things.

Crop circles have also been often associated with UFO sightings. Numerous crop circles have appeared, usually overnight, in fields all over the world. They've been reported since 1975. Most reports have come from England and particularly south-central England, the home of many megaliths (structures made with big stones) erected between 3200 and 1500 B.C.: temples, standing stones, and Stonehenge (a huge circle of standing stones). A crop circle is a circle of flattened crops in a farmer's field or, elsewhere, a circle of flattened grass or brush. While crop circles still arise, they have since 1990 been joined by crop patterns. A crop pattern is an immense, complex design of flattened crops/grass/brush which consists of circles, rings, spirals, triangles, and ladders that are connected to one another by lines. The patterns are characterized as pictograms. Two pictograms happen repeatedly, the 'dumbbell' and the 'insect'. A colossal crop pattern appeared in England on July 7, 1996. It was a 915 foot by 508foot logarithmic spiral filling nearly an acre. The spiral was made up of 151 circles, each of them being six to more than sixty feet in diameter.

Before ending this discussion, it is desirable to reflect upon the levels of science's knowing about things. On page 20, we indicated science's knowledge takes the form of generalizations (principles) and that its generalizations (its knowledge) are considered tentative. Next, we said on pages 20 and 21 that science's goal is to explain all thing in nature. Finally, on page 21, it was indicated that before science can have an explanatory knowledge about things it must have a descriptive knowledge about them and that before it can have a descriptive knowledge about them it needs to have an existential knowledge about these things. Thus, there are three interdependent levels of knowing about a thing: it exists, its description (if it exists), and its explanation (if it has been described). When it comes to UFOs and phenomena related to them, our knowledge is still only existential. A seemingly immovable obstacle to describing and ultimately explaining these phenomena is they're not, so far, being amenable to systematic observation, let alone controlled systematic observation.

Debunkers work hard to undermine the credibility of people who report UFOs and UFO-related phenomena. This they do by stating or intimating that these people didn't see what they said they saw because they misidentified it, are impressionable, under the influence of alcohol or drugs, playing hoaxes, mentally ill, etc. Too much evidence for the existence of these phenomena has accumulated over the last seventy years for us to accept the tirades of debunkers that they do not exist! They do exist, and our government and foreign governments know they do.

2. Ancient legends/myths

Definitions of legend and myth make it difficult to tell them apart. I will therefore treat them as being the same in what follows. Also I will arbitrarily settle on employing the word legend. Basically, a legend is a story that has been circulating a long time and tells of specific events or people we know little or nothing about, except what the story tells us. Ancient legends are legends traceable to ancient times (i.e., between 3500 B.C. and 400 A.D). Some evolved from prehistoric legends, which arose in prehistoric times (i.e., prior to 3500 B.C.). Numerous ancient legends have come down to us in the form of documents.

I will look at research inspired by ancient legends that has been done by Heinrich Schliemann, William Ryan and Walter Pitman, Immanuel Velikovsky, and Zecharia Sitchin. Schliemann as well as Ryan and Pitman wanted to determine whether certain legends are true. Velikovsky and Sitchin wanted to use legends they presumed true to assemble their respective views. We begin with Schliemann.

Schliemann was a German archaeologist of the late 1800s. He became intrigued with legends about two ancient cities, Troy and Mycenae, that were focal points of the Iliad. Now the Iliad is one of two epic poems, the other being the Odyssey, composed by the Greek poet Homer about 800 B.C., the beginning of ancient Greece. Both poems are syntheses of legends that bards had told and retold for centuries of events associated with a war spasmodically fought between Troy in northwestern Turkey and Mycenae in southern Greece from 1192 to 1183 B.C. Said war, the Trojan War, was finally won by the Mycenaens. The Iliad is about the war itself and what led to it whereas the Odyssey tells of the Greek war hero Odysseus' bizarre journey, after the war, back to his home on the island of Ithaca in the Ionian Sea (between Greece and southern Italy). The poems were put into their written form about 750 B.C., shortly after Greeks adopted a modified version of Phoenician writing.

During the early 1870s, Schliemann employed locations mentioned in the Iliad to locate and excavate a by then deeply buried Troy, making its legend a fact. In the late 1870s he again used locations in the Iliad to also find and excavate Mycenae, thereby establishing its factualness. One wonders if the cities would have ever been unearthed had they not been legendary. Schliemann's research was straightforward. There were two legends, they were made into hypotheses, and the hypotheses were confirmed by observation (by observing artifacts imbedded in the geological strata at his excavation sites in Troy and Mycenae).

Straightforward, too, was the research performed by the American marine geologists Ryan and Pitman during the late 1900s. The legend in their case was actually several similar legends about a great flood (page 55). It is best known from the Bible's Book of Genesis, which gives the Jewish legend of the Flood/Deluge. This legend is based on a much older, much longer Sumerian legend about a great flood. According to Archbishop Ussher, met on page 56, the biblical Flood/Deluge took place in 2400 B.C. But according to Sumerian legend it happened before 3000 B.C. The Sumerian version appears in The Epic of Gilgamesh, Gilgamesh being a legendary king of Sumer around 2900 B.C. While the Jewish/biblical legend says the flood was global, the Sumerian one does not say or hint at this. Perhaps the biblical flood was only regional.

So thought Ryan and Pitman (2000) after analyzing sediment in cores removed from the floor of the Mediterranean Sea during the late 1900s. In their book they paint an interesting picture of the way this regional flood occurred. It is as follows.

The last glacial period, or ice age, slowly drew to a close between 12,500 and 9500 B.C. (i.e., between 14,500 and 11,500 years ago). As it did, water from melting glaciers swelled existing rivers and lakes and created new ones. Upon reaching their capacities, lakes overflowed to create more new rivers, some of which created more new lakes. All of this river and lake water was freshwater. Rivers not flowing into lakes flowed into the oceans, whose water was saltwater. From 10,500 to 5500 B.C., oceans and their seas began to gradually rise. Important to the Ryan-Pitman hypothesis is the rising water in the Mediterranean Sea and, particularly, in that section of it called the Aegean Sea (between Turkey and Greece).

Now around 5500 B.C. water in the northeastern Aegean Sea commenced spilling over a low spot along a mountain ridgeline separating what today is Asian Turkey from European Turkey (you might want to look at an atlas). In a matter of weeks, the volume of water flowing over the low spot grew rapidly due to the force of this water lowering and widening the spot more and more. The water cascaded down a steep mountain slope on the other side of the rising Aegean with a deafening roar that could be heard for miles, At the bottom of this slope, 350 feet beneath the Aegean, the cascading water quickly fanned out across the floor of a very large valley and began to fill an already large lake near the center of the valley floor. Within two years, the freshwater lake had doubled in size to become the saltwater sea we know today as the Black Sea.

Judging from our knowledge of prehistoric cultures in the Middle East from 8000 to 4000 B.C., it would appear safe to assume that before the lake became the Black Sea it had attracted to its shores many peoples from nearby eastern Europe, western Asia, and northern Turkey. They may have commenced migrating there about 8500 B.C. After arriving, they replaced their former roving, hunter-gatherer ways of life with the more settled lifestyles of farmers, herders, and fishermen. The transition to sedentary living involved creating new duties/social roles. By 6000 B.C., there could have been 100,000 people living in settlements within ten miles of the lake's very long shoreline. A few communities might have been big enough to be small cities. But since any communities that once existed are buried beneath many feet of sediment lying 200 feet underneath the water, we will probably never find them.

Their research estimated that the great regional flood caused by the Aegean Sea pouring into the valley would have caused the valley's lake to rise at an average rate of six inches per day for two years. If this indeed happened, then most people living near the lake would have steadily headed westward, eastward, and southward toward eastern Europe, western Asia, and northern Turkey. Perhaps a generation or two after some had settled in northern Turkey their descendants spread across the rest of Turkey and into Syria and Mesopotamia (Iraq), bringing with them their great grandparents' memories of the flood. Which is how tales of the flood became part of various ancient Middle Eastern cultures. Ryan and Pitman believe that in about 3500 B.C. the countless word-of-mouth stories coalesced into a few uniform stories, or legends. They also think that about 3000 B.C. one of these legends was committed to writing in Sumer, it being in The Epic of Gilgamesh. Sumer is another name for southern Mesopotamia. It is where the earliest known civilization, the Sumerian, blossomed around 3500 B.C.

We next discuss Velikosky and Sitchin. Recall that their interest in ancient legends is using them as means to attain the end of creating a view on nature. Hence the purpose of their research is noticeably different from that of Schliemann and of Ryan and Pitman. The views they created are often termed theories, Velikovsky's celestial cataclysm theory and Sitchin's 12th planet theory. However, they aren't theories/explanations in the eyes of (orthodox) science, which castigates them for being pseudoscientific. I feel that their views qualify as instances of unorthodox science, not of pseudoscience. Also I feel their views became well enough confirmed to qualify as (unorthodox) scientific theories, not hypotheses. My reason for deeming them scientific theories is they are worded in a manner that allows them to be tested by observing and confirming/disconfirming hypotheses deduced from/implied (predicted) by them. Velikovsky's theory was assembled from hundreds of ancient legends from all over the world. Sitchin's theory was pieced together from a mixture of ancient legends and archaeological information.

Immanuel Velikovsky, referred to on page 64, was an American psychoanalyst who gave up his practice to be a biblical historian. A specific interest of his was to learn what caused the various strange calamities discussed in the Jewish Bible (the Christian

Bible's Old Testament). His theory was the culmination of years of research. It was published in 1950 in the book Worlds In Collision.

Velikovsky's celestial cataclysm theory says our solar system was unstable from 1450 to 500 B.C. Its instability was due to a gigantic mass being ejected from Jupiter which swept by the earth around 1450 B.C. As it passed, there were enormous electro-magnetic and gravitational disturbances/interactions between it and earth that triggered terrifying events never before witnessed by humankind. Over the next nearly thousand years the mass repeatedly cut across the orbits of planets in an irregular fashion. Once, about 700 B.C., it passed by Mars and caused Mars to momentarily veer off course and fly by earth. This flyby gave rise to another batch of scary events on earth. About 500 B.C., stability was restored when the mass settled into a regular orbit around the sun in what was then an empty space between the orbits of earth and Mercury, becoming the planet Venus. Velikovsky felt these cataclysmic celestial events, especially the ones in about 700 B.C., were so awesome that they led to the many legends he uncovered around the world. Ironically, despite him incurring the wrath of scientists in the 1950s and into the 1960s, a few things he said were later confirmed by them. Examples include Venus having a much, much higher average annual ground temperature than scientists in 1950 had thought; Venus rotating on its axis in a direction opposite to that of all other planets in the solar system, something scientists again did not know as of 1950; earth possessing a magnetosphere, unknown in 1950; and radio-frequency noise emissions from Jupiter, which in 1950 were yet to be discovered.

Our solar system formed 4.5 billion years ago. Then 4.0 billion years ago, according to American scholar Zecharia Sitchin, a celestial body far outside the solar system was gravitationally drawn towards and into it. Thus begins Sitchin's 12th planet theory, published in 1976 and subsequently elaborated upon in seven books collectively titled The Earth Chronicles. Sitchin died in 2010, a few years after finishing the seventh book. I will, below, take my best shot at summarizing his intricate theory.

His theory can be construed as four sub-theories: creation of earth, creation of life on earth, creation of our species of human, and creation of our species first civilization. We have already gotten started discussing his idea on how earth was created. So, let us resume that discussion.

The celestial body drawn by gravity into our solar system was about four times larger than earth would be. It crossed the orbit of what 4.0 billion years ago was the solar system's outermost planet (Neptune). Next, it cut across the orbits of the second outermost planet (Uranus), third outermost planet (Saturn), and fourth outermost planet (Jupiter). While crossing their orbits the celestial body added to its moons a few of their moons, through gravitational attraction. In the process, gravity slung one of the moons orbiting Saturn into an orbit well beyond Neptune and thereby made that moon the new outermost planet, tiny Pluto.

Between the orbits of Jupiter and Mars the celestial body headed on a collision course with a planet which 4.0 billion years ago lay between Jupiter and Mars, a planet twice the size earth would be. Although the body brushed the planet it did not collide with the planet. However, many of the body's roughly dozen moon did collide with this planet, obliterating it. About half of the obliterated planet's debris became asteroids in a belt lying between Jupiter and Mars, today's asteroid belt. The other half of the debris became earth and earth's moon, both being catapulted into the previously empty space in between the orbits of Mars and Venus. Meanwhile the celestial body raising all this havoc continued along its course essentially unscathed. Soon it slowly turned and headed again across the paths of Jupiter, Saturn, Uranus, Neptune, and (now) Pluto and hack into the far reaches of space.

Then 3600 years later the celestial body returned. For it had become gravitationally locked into and, as a result, another planet of our solar system. It was the solar system's tenth planet. The tenth planet had an elliptical orbit, as did the other nine planets. But unlike them its orbit was exceedingly elliptical, causing it to spend roughly 80% of its time traveling beyond Pluto's orbit. This means that every 3600 years it fairly quickly crosses the orbits of Pluto, Neptune, Uranus, Saturn, and Jupiter and then, midway between the orbits of Jupiter and Mars, retraces its path back across the orbits of Jupiter, Saturn, Uranus, Neptune, and Pluto and back into the great beyond.

Now the ancient Sumerians living in Sumer (southern Mesopotamia/southern Iraq) came to know of the tenth planet. Yet they considered it the twelfth planet because they had already identified eleven other celestial bodies as planets: Mercury, Venus, earth, Mars, Jupiter, Saturn, Uranus, Neptune, Pluto, the sun, and the moon.

They named the twelfth planet Nibiru (later renamed Marduk) and even gave a name to the obliterated planet, the name Tiamat.

So, earth (and its moon) was created out of a large debris cloud of rock, dust, and gases which was the aftermath of the former planet Tiamat, situated between Mars and Jupiter, being impaled by moons of a newcomer to our solar system, Nibiru, four billion years ago and thus half a billion years after the solar system had formed. This event was also the basis for the creation of future life on earth. In the debris cloud were molecules of life-forms on Nibiru that had been swept off its surface and out of its atmosphere as it brushed Tiamat and which became part of what would be earth's atmosphere. Poetically put, Nibiru seeded (planted life-giving seeds on) earth. Scientists say that by 0.5 billion years ago the earth had a wide variety of fairly simple multi-celled plants and animals. Also, they say 2.5 million years ago the first primitive species of human (Homo habilis) made its debut and that 800, 000 years ago the first advanced species of human (Homo erectus) arrived on the scene,

The theory indicates life had flourished on Nibiru since at least five billion years ago and that by the time Tiamat was obliterated a very advanced species of human inhabited Nibiru. This species was by that time as technologically sophisticated as our species is now. Four billion years ago, members of the species-the Nibirueans- keenly observed and carefully recorded the catastrophe unfolding in the sky above Nibiru. As an aside, Sitchin says the Sumerians existed 200,000 years ago, knew of the Nibirueans, referred to Nibirueans living on earth as Anunnaki, and eventually learned all this and much more from their Anunnaki overseers.

Nibirueans became increasingly familiar with our solar system from four billion years ago onward as Nibiru journeyed once every 3600 years from Pluto to midway between Jupiter and Mars and then back to Pluto. Their technology enabled them to learn much without leaving Nibiru, by using remote-sensing devices on Nibiru or by unmanned remotely controlled spacecraft (drones) equipped with sensors. At times the information acquired in this way led to manned spacecraft flying above or even landing on a planet so that Nibireans could learn more. It was 445,000 years ago, according to Sitchin, that the Nibirueans flew to and landed on earth. Their mission was to find tons of gold and send it back to Nibiru to remedy a worsening environmental problem there. The Nibirneans splashed down in the Persian Gulf, established a mission control center in Sumer, and began scouting the world in search of gold. Rich deposits were found in southeast Africa. A mining operation was started there and Nibirueans were brought from Nibiru to work in the African gold mines. Before long, gold was being mined in Africa, taken by sea in barges to Sumer, refined, flown from a spaceport in Sumer in fairly small craft to holding facilities on Mars, and flown from Mars in larger spacecraft to Nibiru, where the refined gold was ground into a powder and dispersed into the Nibiruean atmosphere.

Despite the sophistication of their technology, Nibiruean/Anunnaki miners suffered great hardship mining gold. Unrest among them shortly led to mutiny. The person in charge of the mining operation sympathized with their suffering and told them he had an idea that would end it. This individual, named Enki, told the nurse who was providing medical care at the mining camp to help him turn the idea into a reality. His idea was to genetically reengineer into a miner an advanced species of human, Homo erectus, dwelling in east Africa that Annunaki/Nibirueans had observed and casually studied for many years. Research got underway. The feat was accomplished 300,000 years ago, a hybrid creature having mostly Homo erectus genes and a few Anunnaki genes. Unfortunately, its genetic makeup needed fine tuning in order for it to reproduce. Reproduction was not achieved until 250,000 years ago. That's when a still more advanced species of human, Homo sapiens (us), was created and replaced the Anunnaki (those Nibirueans on earth) in the mines. Thus our species was created by Anunnaki to serve Anunnaki.

Anunnaki lived for hundreds of thousands of years. For instance, Enki was mature enough to be leader of the reconnaissance team which 445,000 years ago splashed down in the Persian Gulf. He was still alive 250,000 years ago when our species was created, 13,000 years ago when the last glacial period drew to a close, and 5500 years ago when our first civilization was created. If so, then he could still be alive. Anunnaki appeared immortal to us. That, along with their superior knowledge and abilities, made them also seem like gods to us, although the Anunnaki did not view themselves as gods (Sitchin indicates they believed in a superior being somewhat like God). Now a little Anunnakian/Nibiruean longevity was instilled in early members of our species, probably the result of children born of intercourse between Anunnaki men and Homo sapiens women. However, it dwindled from 13,000 to 11,000 years ago, dropping on average from 900 years old to 80 years old.

Sitchin talks about a global flood which took place 13,000 years ago and wiped out nearly all of humanity. But this is not relevant to the four sub-theories being discussed.

I will therefore skip his interesting account of the flood and go to his fourth sub-theory, creation of our species' first civilization.

Except for high mountains forming its northern border with Turkey, Mesopotamia is a flat land not much above sea level. Now the flood had consisted of an immense tidal wave preceded by torrential rain. The flood and the generally rainier weather that began at the end of the last ice age made Mesopotamia's extensive lowlands into a largely uninhabitable marsh until 7000 years ago (5000 B.C.). It was about 5000 B.C. that people living for millennia in the northern mountains commenced to slowly move in growing numbers down from them to the lowland plains and engage in larger-scale agriculture. Prior to the flood, Anunnaki considered humans their servants. After the flood, they started to treat people with a little more respect and to help them make it through their austere stay in the mountains to which they had fled the flood. Anunnaki became more interested inthem as they left the mountains for the plains. In fact, between 5000 and 4000 B.C. both Anunnaki and humans worked on a joint land-reclamation project. Its purpose was to rebuild eight Anunnakian 'cities', better characterized as settlements, in Sumer/southern Mesopotamia devastated by the flood, to build about a dozen new ones there, and to create hundreds of parcels of irrigated farmland for humans.

Around 3600 B.C., Anunnaki ruling the rebuilt cities in Sumer began to increasingly appoint humans to administer their cities. These administrators were termed kings. About 3500 B.C., Anunnaki commenced teaching humans the things they need to know to create and maintain a civilization (a civilized society): government, law, education, morality, literature, medicine, technology, science. The result was our species' first civilization, the Sumerian civilization (3500-2400 B.C.). It was followed in Sumer by the Akkadian civilization (2265-1950 B.C.), Babylonian/Amorite civilization (1950-1670 B.C.), etc. Also the Anunnaki told Sumerians more about themselves, meaning the Anunnaki, and about the creations of earth, life, and humans. This information was recorded by Sumerians on hundreds of clay tablets, initially as pictograms and next in the more useful form of cuneiform writing.

So much for Sitchin's theory. What is one to make of it? The legends he cites to justify his theory are not usually interpreted by him the way scholars have traditionally interpreted them. This has led many scholars who specialize in ancient languages and texts to claim Sitchin has a superficial understanding of most of the legends because he has a poor grasp of most of the languages in which they were originally written. My feeling is that the legends justify most aspects of his theory as long as knowledgeable people find his unique interpretation of the legends to be reasonable. As of now, all I can say is time will tell. Personally, Sitchin's theory fascinates me.

3. Psychic phenomena

Psychic phenomena, frequently abbreviated 'psi', are also known as paranormal phenomena and parapsychological phenomena. Psychic phenomena have four things in common with UFOs and UFO-related phenomena. First, some people say they exist; others say they do not exist and that what's termed a psychic phenomenon is in truth a misperception (illusion), hoax, hallucination, or delusion. Second, they are nonmaterial and thus neither matter nor energy derived from matter. Third, such psychic phenomena as telepathy and materializations/dematerializations are often associated with UFOs and UFO-related phenomena. Fourth, they are difficult to confirm by means of systematic observation, be it the naturalistic systematic observation done in naturalistic research or the controlled systematic observation done in experimental research (page 31).

Parapsychology is a branch of psychology which studies psychic phenomena. It has identified and classified many kinds. My discussion concentrates on seven of them: telepathy, clairvoyance (including clairaudience), out-of-body experiences (astral projection), precognition, psychokinesis, psychic healing, and channeling (mediumship).

Telepathy has as synonyms mental telepathy, which is redundant, and thought trans ference, which is more descriptive albeit less impressive. It is the transfer of thoughts, or information, from one mind to another without using any of the known senses (i.e., the sensory processes of seeing, hearing, touching, smelling, tasting, sensing pain, sensing temperature, sensing bodily position, etc.). Hence telepathy is a non-sensory perceptual process. This is why it is viewed as one instance of extrasensory perception (ESP), two other instances of ESP being clairvoyance/clairaudience and out-of-body experiences. Now in telepathy the communication, transmission, or transfer of a thought from one person's mind to another person's mind seems instantaneous and to therefore take no time. Telepathy can be between a living person and a dead person. If a medium facilitates such telepathy by acting as a go-between, then telepathy is usually dubbed channeling (discussed last).

Quality of telepathic communication depends upon the mental states of the people engaged in it, more so the receiver than the transmitter of a telepathic message/thought. Telepathy, like most psychic phenomena, is very subtle. Its messages are nearly always fairly weak and occur within a context of fairly strong disruptive mental activity. For readers acquainted with electronic signal detection systems, the challenge the recipient of a telepathic message faces is akin to such a system trying to detect a comparatively weak signal immersed within a background of relatively strong noise. Which may be the reason telepathic messages are more easily detected and accurately interpreted by a recipient when he/she either is awake yet relaxed or is asleep. Messages received while asleep are examples of what is called dream telepathy. A lot was learned about dream telepathy in the late 1960s and early 1970s at the Maimonides Medical Center's Dream Laboratory in Brooklyn, New York.

Clairvoyance and clairaudience, two French words, refer to a person being able to clearly see things (clairvoyance) or clearly hear things (clairaudience) without using eyes or ears. Both differ from telepathy, which involves two people communicating with one another. The sights seen/sounds heard can originate at locations from a few feet to three thousand miles away from the clairvoyant/clairaudient, as can the telepathic contact between a transmitter and a receiver. Unlike the typically split-second thought that occurs in telepathy, the sights/sounds perceived in clairvoyance/clairaudience ordinarily flow as if the percipient were watching/hearing a movie or television show. The descriptions of what it was a person perceived at a location have frequently been verified by subsequent interviews with people at the location at the time the person perceived it. Clairaudience seems rarer than clairvoyance. Thus clairvoyance has been better documented. Many experiments were performed in the mid 1900s to test people's clairvoyant ability by observing how often they identified the image (e.g., a star, a wavy line, a square, etc.) on the backs of a well shuffled deck of ESP cards. The average person did no better, or only a little better, than would be expected if chance alone had governed her choices. A few people did five or more times better than chance. They were considered to be definitely clairvoyant.

Out-of-body experiences (OOBEs or OBEs) are also known as astral projection and traveling clairvoyance. In an OOBE a person sees or occasionally hears what is happening at a location and is fully aware of being there. Frequently one or more people at the scene are conscious of the projected person's presence there and sometimes may see him, hear him, and touch him. What is it they see, hear, or touch? It is a three-dimensional nonmaterial replica of him that is termed his double, duplicate, astral body, or vehicle of vitality. And it consists of a substance which can vary in density. The denser the substance is, the less transparent and more solid the astral body is. A projected person's astral body wears clothes that resemble those worn by the person's physical body. It appears the specific clothes worn by an astral body frequently mirror the specific reason for a person temporarily leaving his physical body. During the time people are outside their physical body they observe a luminous pearly white cord running from the head of their astral body to the head of their physical body. Astral bodies have clairvoyant/clairaudient, telepathic, and psychokinetic abilities. Finally, near-death experiences (NDEs) are OOBEs that happen when a physical body has a medical crisis.

Precognition is knowing what will occur before it occurs, without any point-at-able physical (material) basis for this. The knowledge/information obtained is referred to as a precognition, a premonition, and precognitive knowledge. Like telepathic thoughts, precognitions are experienced as flashes of insight. While insight can take place anytime, it usually happens in a dream.

Psychokinesis is the ability to influence things nearby or far away, again with no known physical basis. It is popularly dubbed mind over matter. All types of things can be so influenced: spoons, photographic film, the weight of objects, a stream of water coming out of a faucet, the direction in which a compass needle points, the strength of the magnetic field being measured by a magnetometer, levitating one's body or something else, etc. Psychokinetic ability seems rare and is less well confirmed than the four previous psychic abilities. Nonetheless, there are reports from credible witnesses of seeing somebody lift off the ground, float awhile through the air, and descend to the ground, all the time never appearing to be uncomfortable, nervous, or panic stricken. Uri Geller is one of the best known psychokinesthetists. His clairvoyant and precognitive abilities are well known too.

Psychic healing is one person, a healer, helping another person, a patient, overcome a bodily affliction, a spiritual affliction, or both. It is the least understood and most controversial of psychic phenomena. Many charlatans saying they possess this ability have been exposed. A bona fide psychic healer strives to diagnose and treat a malady. She, or he is not only successful at healing most patients seen but heals them faster and for much less money than is the case with practitioners of conventional/established/accepted/mainstream/orthodox medicine. Two respected psychic healers were America's Edger Casey (1877-1945) and Brazil's Arigo (1918-1971).

Channeling has had its hucksters too. It began as a practice known as mediumship, so named because a person called a medium (more accurately, a mental medium) made it possible. Actually, mediumship and mediums existed during ancient times. Back then they were called prophesy and prophets. Jews in Canaan (Palestine) had many prophets between 800 and 500 B.C., each of them giving to the Jewish nation messages he had received from God. And the Greeks between 600 and 200 B.C. had a few oracle-givers, people who gave to an individual an oracle received from a Greek god. Oracle meant a message to an individual from a god (e.g., Apollo). Also, it meant a sacred location in Greece (e.g., Delphi) where divine messages were heard. Now the word medium, in the sense it is being used here, was coined around 1850.

Mediums serve as channels through which information from disincarnate souls (i.e., souls without physical bodies) flows to incarnate souls (i.e., souls with physical bodies, and thus people that are alive). Therefore, a medium functions as a go-between, linking unembodied souls to embodied souls. Since the late 1970s, the link a medium provides has been increasingly termed a channel. This has led to mediums/mediumship being referred to as channels/channeling. How does mediumship work?

Basically, a person gets in touch with a medium and asks to have a séance (sitting) with her/him, at which the medium will contact a deceased friend or family member of the person who the person wants to talk to. The séance will ordinarily commence by the medium entering a trance (an altered state of consciousness), although a few mediums do not need to do this. After going into the trance and contacting the deceased individual, the medium will speak for the deceased using thoughts telepathically transmitted by the deceased. A conversation will ensue in which the person asking for the séance asks the deceased questions and the deceased answers them, utilizing the medium's voice (which may sound slightly different than before the trance). The séance will normally last one to two hours and end when the medium regains her waking-state consciousness, whereupon she will seldom remember what was said during the séance. Occasionally, two or more people attend a séance and take turns questioning the deceased.

References

Avey, Albert R. Handbook In The History Of Philosophy. New York: Barnes & Noble, 1961 (second edition).

Mack, John E. Passport To The Cosmos. New York: Crown Publishers, 1999 (fairly hard). Thought-provoking impressions of an abductee hypnotherapist regarding the human abduction phenomenon.

Mitchell, Edgar D. Psychic Exploration. New York: G.P. Putnam's Sons, 1974 (fairly easy). A highly recommended introduction to psychic phenomena, its 29 chapters being written by 29 authors well known and respected in parapsychology at the time.

Ryan, William and Pitman, Walter Noah's Flood. New York: Touchstone, 2000 (fairly easy).

Sitchin, Zecharia The 12th Planet. Rochester (Vermont): Bear & Company, 1991 (fairly hard) [originally published by Stein and Day of New York in 1976]

Sitchin, Zecharia Genesis Revisited. Rochester (Vermont): Bear & Company, 1991 (fairly hard). [originally published by Avon Books of New York in 1990]

Thompson, Richard L. Alien Identities. Badger (California): Govardhan Hill, 1993 (fairly easy). An interesting comparison of modern UFOs and their humanoids with ancient Hindu legends about vimanas (aircraft) and their humanoids.

Velikovsky, Immanuel Worlds In Collision (1965 edition). New York: Quality Paperback Book Club, 1997 (fairly easy).

CHAPTER 7

Science And Religion

Our coverage in Chapter 4 of scientific and nonscientific views on nature showed friction has existed in modern times between science and religion. In this chapter, I'll give my opinions on how the two can maybe coexist on better terms. From the outset, you are cautioned to not equate science with modern humanism (page 30). Science, like religion, is a social institution. Modern humanism is not. It is a philosophy of life that adopts science as the chief means of attaining its end, which is for a society to encourage and help all its citizens realize their potential and thereby achieve fulfillment. (Modern) humanism looks up to science and down at religion. Its reverence for science is known as, usually with derision, scientism. It is important to know that humanism is not embraced by scientists, as a group. Consequently, it would be wrong to assume a scientist is a humanist. Nonetheless many scientists are humanists. Scientists that are humanists are characteristically either atheists (i.e., people who do not believe God exists) or agnostics (i.e., people who do not believe God's existence or nonexistence is knowable). This tends to put them at odds with scientists that are theists (i.e., people who believe that God exists), especially those theists who are religious conservatives (i.e., fundamentalists and evangelicals among Christians and the orthodox among Jews and Muslims).

Another caution is in order. People are often imprecise in how they say things. A common imprecision is talking in generalizations. One generalization heard is there is friction between science and religion. Taken at face value, or literally, this means there is largely friction between most scientists and most religious people over most topics dear to both. Exactly what do people saying this mean? Do they intend it to be taken at face value? If they do, then they ought to be able to back their statement with sufficient, reasonably accurate evidence concerning what scientists and religious people have said or with evidence of similar quality concerning what they personally have observed. If they are not able to do this, then they ought not make the generalization.

Talking in generalizations that are not true or whose truth is not known or is poorly known can set fires and fan the flames of existing fires. Some individuals employ such generalizations as means to ends which are not the ends that others are led to think they are. Assume I am a social activist. My activities and self-image are legitimate only as long as my cause exists, and my cause exists only as long as the social problem motivating it exists. I know the problem will endure if my actions do not solve it, thus allowing my cause to endure. Of course, I cannot tell this to others (perhaps not even to myself) and will try convincing them (and maybe myself) that my actions will solve the problem or at least stop it from worsening. But my actions will actually prolong the problem by decreasing, not increasing, the chances of people in two clashing groups mixing with and thereby getting to better know, like, and respect each other (thereby solving or lessening the problem). Something I might do to keep the groups apart is to utter a questionable generalization designed to do just that. The illustration can be extended to people other than social activists, such as some people who claim there is friction between science and religion. What are they trying to achieve by saying this?

Now there is friction between science and religion. It takes the form of differences between their views on nature and between the methods they use to arrive at these views. However, I do not think this friction is as much as some people would have us think it is. Most people that talk about it fall into two camps. One camp is religious conservatives, who started growing in number about 1900. The other camp is humanists, who began to grow in number around 1925. The book by Gary Ferngren (2002) in the References of Chapter 4 is a balanced account on the relationship between science and religion. So is a book by Ian Barbour (1966), which in spite of its age is still illuminating. A clearly less balanced book on the relationship is by Paul Kurtz (2003). It gives largely the humanist position on the relationship. Parenthetically, 15 out of its 37 contributors are members of the Committee for the Scientific Investigation of Claims of the Paranormal (CSICP), referred to on pages 63 and 65.

When and where did friction between science and religion arise? It arose during the 1100s in Roman Catholic Europe (all of Europe except southeast Europe). That is when and where there came to be a sudden awareness of ancient Greek and medieval Moslem knowledge about nature and other subjects (page 49). Said knowledge posed a serious threat to the Catholic Church's image of omniscience and goaded the Church into embracing Aristotelianism or, to be more accurate, Thomism (i.e., Saint Thomas Aquinas' version of Aristotle's philosophy) in order to preserve its intellectual authority. Part of Aristotelian philosophy was natural philosophy, which is today termed science.

Relations between science and religion in Catholic Europe were friction-free from the time the Church adopted Aristotelianism in the late 1200s until about 1600, when the Church started denouncing Copernicus' heliocentric theory (page 50). Now until 1600 the strength of the Church assured that there would be ne friction between science and religion, it having the power to decide and to enforce what is and is not a theologically acceptable scientific view of nature.

From 1520 to 1650, Europe was buffeted by religious tumult as one group of protestors after another that were dedicated to reforming Christianity split from the Catholic Church and established Protestant denominations in what was to be called the Protestant Reformation. An urge for religious reconciliation and tolerance commenced growing in England among Christian intellectuals, especially natural philosophers, during the early 1600s. It led in the mid 1600s to a religious alternative to Catholicism and Protestantism called natural theology (religion).

Natural theology largely minimized revealed theology and, consequently, was not seen by most Catholics and Protestants as Christian theology. It sidestepped the thorny issues separating Catholicism and Protestantism and bought religious harmony at the expense of reducing Christianity to a belief in God, the soul's immortality, and a need for moral conduct. Natural theology emphasized God the Creator (who as time passed was called the Designer, Architect, Artificer, and Clockmaker) and it deemphasized God the Redeemer and Christ the Way (to redemption). It said that after God created the universe/nature He mostly let it run on its own, meaning under the influence of natural laws He had created, and that his subsequent involvement was limited to sometimes adjusting these laws (thus the expression 'God of the gaps') and occasionally performing miracles. In the early 1700s, natural theology gave rise to deism. It stated that although God still exists He no longer bridges gaps or performs miracles. Deism lost its appeal in the mid 1700s; natural theology lost its appeal in the early 1800s. My guess is that most of the loss in their popularity resulted from well-educated people steadily becoming atheists and agnostics who, like the philosophes in the Age of Reason (page 30), looked to science for acquiring knowledge and fulfillment.

The Age of Reason petered out about 1790 after going as far as it could to shape outlooks. By 1800, its influence and that of science and technology had helped to reduce the intense religious turmoil of 150 years earlier and had begun to redirect a growing number of people's interest from the hereafter to the here-and-now, making many conservative Christians more moderate and some moderate Christians more liberal. Between 1750 and 1850, science was tolerated by most Christian denominations (sects) and even encouraged by a few Protestant ones. This gave it a better chance to grow from an activity into the social institution it became around 1850.

Christianity's toleration of science commenced being strained during the mid 1800s with the debuts of Lyell's theory of geological evolution and particularly Darwin's theory of biological evolution (page 57). To these two tensions attributable to science, the first since Galileo's time, was added a third. It was a German scholarly pursuit called biblical criticism and the Higher Criticism that arose in about 1790 and grew rapidly after 1850. Its purpose was to validate passages in the Bible, meaning to learn their linguistic and historic bases. The tools used to do this were philology (the study of languages), logic, archaeology, and history. Biblical criticism's scholars made a major discovery in the late 1800s and early 1900s: inconsistencies in passages of the Jewish Bible, which is the Old Testament of the Christian Bible, were found to be due to priests assembling it from several sources of information the scholars call source documents (all long gone). Four sources were heavily relied upon and were termed by these scholars the Yahwist (or J), Elohist (E), Deuteronomist (D), and Priestly (P) documents. Beginning about 1900, conservative American Christians heard of this work in Germany and felt that it threatened the foundation of their faith. Christians elsewhere were not as concerned because most of them were moderate Christians (page 69).

Protestant fundamentalists and evangelicals in America were the primary defenders and promoters of Christianity in America during the 1900s. They were, and still are, a force to be dealt with in conflicts between science and religion. We have already said a lot about fundamentalists (pages 58, 59, and 69). One more remark will now he made. Fundamentalism employs a two-pronged approach to defend and promote Christianity. One prong is insisting on accepting as literally true everything the Bible says. The other is eliminating contrary views, be they secular or religious, through promotional literature and speakers and through political activism. A big secular target of fundamentalism has been science, especially biology, and particularly Darwinian evolution, though areas in geology and paleontology whose research or theories have lent credence to Darwinism have come under the gun too.

How can science and religion coexist on better terms? The foregoing suggests that we reword our question to address where most friction really lies. So instead let us ask: how can humanists on the one hand and conservative Christians, Jews, and Muslims on the other hand coexist on better terms? I have four ideas.

First, humanists and religious conservatives should fully realize that what they are disagreeing about are their respective worldviews (page 49). Second, when they lament the alleged ill effects on society of an opposing worldview, humanists and religious conservatives should not dismiss as ridiculous the possible adverse social effects of their own worldview. Third, humanist scientists applying religious terms outside a religious con-text and inside a scientific one, as when they say they are searching for the Holy Grail or the God particle, should realize that such references, while maybe intended to stimulate public curiosity or be seen by fellow humanists as metaphors reflecting unabashed excitement, are taken by many religious people, and not only religious conservatives, as being insensitive to them and trivializing their faith. The fourth idea addresses the religious conservatives in Christianity, Judaism, and Islam. Their faith is based on a book deemed inspired by the Word of God: the Christian Bible, the Jewish Bible, and the Koran. I express my idea within a Christian setting.

The pastor of my church occasionally says in sermons that "Bible' is an acronym for Basic Instruction Before Leaving Earth. It seems quite appropriate, since the purpose of the Bible is to allow souls after death to reside in Heaven. Now in order for the Bible to accomplish this it must cover all spiritual bases associated with our terrestrial existence that have a bearing on a subsequent heavenly existence. In other words, it must give us the tools (i.e., a knowledge about conditions necessary and sufficient) for our souls to get from here to there. Also to accomplish its mission the Bible must furnish a context for what it says by painting a big picture of existence whose details are mission-relevant and intelligible to people God intended to receive the biblical message. The context is given in the Bible's first book, Genesis. For the Bible to be comprehended by people receiving it, its concepts had to dovetail with what they knew about nature and therefore with their scientific and technological knowledge, which when compared to today's was very crude. The Bible would have lost credibility in the eyes of its intended audience, early Jews, and failed in its purpose had it said in Genesis what we know today about nature. So instead, it said things that conformed to what Jews knew, thus making what it said understandable to them. This is what parents do when they explain things to a preschool child.

Where am I going with this? Assume that evolution as conceived by Darwin, or anybody else for that matter, were true. How could the Bible have told it to people in antiquity in a way they would understand? Or assume the big bang theory about how the universe originated were true. How might the Bible have conveyed it to the ancients so they would be able to grasp it? Each theory presupposes a person learning it has more than a passing acquaintance with the science, biology or astronomy, that created it. We know that many, many species of plants and animals came and went long before humans existed. Should the Bible have mentioned, or not mentioned, at least a few of them, like Tyrannosaurus rex? In ancient times it was believed feelings emotions - well up in the heart. Contemporary scientific evidence points to them arising in the brain, although a few of us when in love may say they emanate from their heart. Should the Bible have corrected or, as it did, accepted and used the ancient belief feelings arise in the heart? If it contradicted tradition by asserting they are generated in the brain, then this could have unduly risked its credibility in what it wanted people to believe. Delving more than it did into nature would have probably sabotaged the Bible's purpose.

And my fourth idea? It is for conservative Christians to become moderate Christians. That would noticeably lessen clashes between Christians and humanists and thus the friction between religion and science. Moving from a conservative to a moderate stance requires admitting the Bible has passages that are vague, inconsistent, or in error. Also, it requires allowing onto religious turf people with the skill and desire to identify the Bible's errors and possibly rectify them. This means that biblical criticism scholars and scientists ought to be welcomed, not shunned. I think the result would be not only more harmony but a better understanding of God. Now if God had waited until today to give us information in the Bible then His message would have likely been different insofar as the words and concepts used, making it more resonant with today's scientific knowledge. This does not mean the message would agree with everything that science now accepts as probably true. After all, science is a work in progress. Moreover, in spite of science's impressive track record over the last four centuries, I am not about to think that science will someday be able to explain or even describe all of nature. Nor does the foregoing mean that his message would disagree with everything that science currently holds to be probably true.

References

Barbour, Ian G. Issues in Science and Religion. Englewood Cliffs (N.J.): Prentice-Hall, 1966 (hard).

Callahan, Tim Secret Origins Of The Bible. Altadena (California): Millennium Press, 2002 (hard). This is a fine example of biblical criticism.

Ferngren, Gary B. (Editor) Science & Religion: A Historical Introduction. Baltimore; The Johns Hopkins University Press, 2002 (fairly easy).

Haisch, Bernard The God Theory. San Francisco: Weiser Books, 2006 (hard). He is an Astrophysicist, and his book is intriguing. Its subtitle is Universes, Zero-Point Fields, And What's Behind It All.

Kurtz, Paul (Editor) Science and Religion: Are They Compatible? Amherst (N.Y.): Prometheus Books, 2003 (fairly easy).

Tippler, Frank J. The Physics of Immortality. New York: Doubleday, 1994 (hard). Here a mathematical physicist outlines in detail his thoughts on the physical basis of immortality. This is a unique book.